RETIREMENT IS A
MARATHON

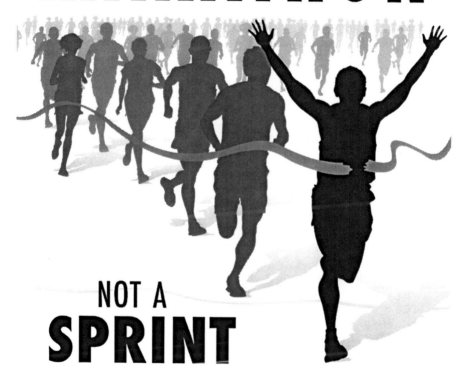

NOT A
SPRINT

CHRIS SCALESE

RETIREMENT IS A
MARATHON

NOT A
SPRINT

A Common Sense Financial Training Guide
to Get You to the Finish Line - Without Hitting the Wall.

Published by Advantage, Charleston, South Carolina.
Member of Advantage Media Group.

ADVANTAGE is a registered trademark and the Advantage colophon is a trademark of Advantage Media Group, Inc.

Printed in the United States of America.

ISBN: 978-159932-307-7
LCCN: 2012936286

This publication is designed to provide accurate and authoritative information in regard to the subject matter covered. It is sold with the understanding that the publisher is not engaged in rendering legal, accounting, or other professional services. If legal advice or other expert assistance is required, the services of a competent professional person should be sought.

Advantage Media Group is proud to be a part of the Tree Neutral® program. Tree Neutral offsets the number of trees consumed in the production and printing of this book by taking proactive steps such as planting trees in direct proportion to the number of trees used to print books. To learn more about Tree Neutral, please visit www.treeneutral.com. To learn more about Advantage's commitment to being a responsible steward of the environment, please visit www.advantagefamily.com/green

Advantage Media Group is a leading publisher of business, motivation, and self-help authors. Do you have a manuscript or book idea that you would like to have considered for publication? Please visit www.amgbook.com or call 1.866.775.1696

Table of Contents

Author's Note

As someone who has spent the last 20 years of my career helping individuals plan their retirement, and as a veteran of over 60 marathons, I have found there are many parallels between retirement planning and marathon training.

Typically, a solid retirement plan is one that has evolved over many years. The most successful retirees I have come across are those who have planned for years and years before getting to the "starting line" of retirement. They have methodically planned and saved with a specific goal in mind. The retirees who struggle financially with their retirement plans are usually those who kind of "wing it." They pick an arbitrary age, like 62 or 66, to retire. Because they have no plan or foundation going into retirement, their retirement is vulnerable to many things outside of their control, such as the stock market and interest rates.

Similarly, the most successful marathon runners that I know train diligently for months and months before they get to the start of their race. They train in all types of conditions and are ready for anything come race day. The runners who struggle the most during their race are those who do very little training and come to the race without a foundation in place.

The most successful retirees are those who look at retirement as a long endeavor that can last 20 or 30 years or longer. They don't throw all of their years of preparation away by investing in the next "hot stock" or investment idea. They're very careful with their finances; they know they have to make sure that their money will last for the rest of their lives. They stay conservative and focused on a finish line that is years and years away. People who struggle in retirement are those who still have a "get rich quick" mentality. Even though they no longer have the comfort of a paycheck coming in, they still put their retirement nest egg at risk by chasing every hot tip that they get. In other words, they are looking for short cuts to bring them financial stability and peace of mind.

To run a successful marathon, you have to practice patience. No matter how good you feel in the early miles, you need to resist the temptation to run too hard. If you make this mistake, you will waste your training and will struggle mightily to reach the finish line. You may have heard the term "hitting the wall." This is a very real phenomenon where the body feels as if it can't go any further. This usually results from running too hard in the early miles so that your body burns through its energy reserves.

In retirement, as in a marathon, you need to realize there is a very long road ahead of you. You need to be patient and trust in the preparation that got you there in the first place. By attempting to deviate from your plan, you may find yourself out of energy—or out of money—well before the finish line.

—Chris Scalese

INTRODUCTION:
A New Way of Looking at Retirement

Would you like to never lose another penny in the stock market?

Would you like to have an income that beats bank returns and is guaranteed to never run out during your or your spouse's lifetime?

Would you like to pay less in taxes?

Would you like to protect your assets from nursing homes without having to buy long-term-care insurance?

You can do all these things, and I will show you how. But first, I want you to think about your retirement in a radically different way.

When most people think about retirement, they look at their 401(k), their IRA, their stocks, bonds and savings, add those numbers up, and think, "Okay, that's how much money I have to fund my retirement." But the total of your assets only tells half the story. Your retirement is funded by the monthly income you can generate from those savings, which is why finding the right investment vehicles and employing tax-reduction (and fee-avoidance) strategies are so important to enjoying your retirement without financial stress. Let me show you what I mean by looking at two retirement marathoners (individuals who have reached the starting line of their retirement marathon).

In lane one, we have someone with a $1,000,000 retirement portfolio, and in lane two, we have someone else with a $600,000 retirement portfolio. On the surface you might say, "The person with the million dollars is in better shape for retirement." Okay, that sounds reasonable, but let's look a little closer. If the guy with the million dollars has it all in CDs, and right now CDs are only paying 1 percent, then he is only generating $10,000 of income a year from that portfolio. And then if he is in the 15 percent tax bracket, for example, then he is only deriving $8,500 from that portfolio after taxes.

Then we take another look at the guy in lane two with $600,000 in assets. If he has his assets in a tax-efficient portfolio that's earning 5 percent a year, he is getting $30,000 a year of income. And if it's very tax-efficient, maybe he is only paying $500 a year in taxes. So this guy is getting $29,500 of after-tax income versus $8,500 of after-tax income. Now who do you think will come out on top? Who is enjoying his retirement more—the person with $29,500 of income, or the person with $8,500 of income?

Always remember that the income you can get is what's going to drive your retirement, not necessarily what your asset level is.

RETIREMENT SHOULD BE A CAUSE FOR CELEBRATION

I'm glad you're reading this book because it means you have been thinking seriously about planning for your retirement. The first thing I say when people tell me they are retired or are retiring soon is "congratulations," because it is a great accomplishment to complete your career. Your retirement years should be spent on those things in life that you and your spouse enjoy. However, you do need to make some changes in your lifestyle to make sure your retirement is as rewarding and fulfilling as you deserve.

The most important thing to understand is that retirement requires a change in mind-set. You're not collecting a regular paycheck anymore, so you need to change how you think about investments, fees and taxes. You should start out by having your retirement plan analyzed. If you are one of the many people out there who doesn't have a plan, the first thing you should do is create one.

Something caused you to pick up this book. There is something you're not happy with that keeps you up at night, and you are trying to find the solution to it. The definition of financial insanity is to keep doing what you're doing, and expecting something different to happen. So many people expect the problem to suddenly go away. But I'm telling you, the problem will not go away on its own. You need to make some changes in what you're doing for that problem to go away, and I want to show you how to make those changes.

A TRUE FINANCIAL PLAN IS NEVER FINISHED

Your financial plan isn't something you set up and then ignore. It really is like a marathon. In a marathon, the race itself changes as your mind and body change. By the time you reach the end, everything seems different. A financial plan also changes as your life changes and your priorities change. You should have a long-term relationship with your professional retirement advisor and communicate with him or her regularly to make sure your plan fits your ever-changing needs. A true financial plan is never finished. It is revisited every year to ensure that it is working to achieve your goals.

REACH YOUR FINANCIAL AND EMOTIONAL GOALS

The financial outcomes you seek can be achieved by working on your financial affairs. But none of those outcomes really matter if they don't help you achieve something emotionally. When I talk to people like you, who are either retired or are getting close to retirement, I think about how hard you've worked over the years to get where you are today. I know that all of you have saved, sacrificed, and have done without through the years to raise and provide for a family.

And now that you are finally able to retire, and the race is finally run, you feel these should truly be your golden years. This is the time that you should be able to slow down and enjoy all the things in life that are important to you. You should finally have time for your hobbies, whether they are fishing, golf, cooking—or running marathons. You should enjoy spending time with the people who are most important to you: your spouse, your children, your grandkids, and your friends. You should be traveling more, if that is something you enjoy.

Your retirement years are not the time to be worrying about your money and lying awake at night asking yourself, *Do I have enough? What is the stock market going to do to my nest egg? What are the government, taxes, and health care costs going to do to my savings?*

You need to have a plan in place that addresses these questions, something that will help you reach your goals, so that you can enjoy the worry-free retirement you deserve. So let's get started.

The Unique Challenges of Retirees

Chapter One

THE AGE OF ANXIETY

Whenever I speak to retirees about the current financial climate, people ask me, "How did we get where we are today?" Suddenly, your marathon seems to be filled with hurdles. People's confidence in retirement planning is at an all-time low right now, and a number of factors have gotten us to this point.

Number one is the stock market. These days, people are more nervous about the stock market than they ever have been. Those people who retired back in the 1980s and 1990s were used to realizing a rate of return somewhere between 8 and 10 percent a year consistently, without having a lot of negative years. That has changed in the past 10 years. Chances are that most investors in the stock market since the 2000s have experienced very little growth because the markets as a whole have not grown much. The lack of consistent returns—not to mention the losses—has caused people to be extremely nervous about their retirement.

Another reason people are nervous is that changes can be made as suggested fixed interest rates are at a historic low right now. Six or seven years ago, if the stock market wasn't cooperating, people figured they could put their money into CDs (or their equivalents) and get anywhere from a 4 to a 5 percent return on their money, without putting their principal at risk. Well, 4 to 5 percent is an acceptable rate of return, so even when the market wasn't producing, people had reasonable alternatives. But with CDs hovering at 1 percent or lower, that option is not as viable anymore.

The third reason for anxiety about retirement is that fewer and fewer employers are offering defined pension programs for their employees. What do I mean here? A defined pension program is when you work "X" amount of years for an employer, and in return, they tell you, "Okay, based on your years of service, we'll pay you $1,000 a month for life, or $1,500 a month for life, or $2,000 a month for life." As recently as 20 years ago, roughly 80 percent of retirees had pensions. Today, based on the people I talk to, I estimate that only 20 to 30 percent of people have that kind of pension. With all these factors—stock market volatility, low CD rates, and pensions disappearing—it's no wonder that people are nervous about their retirement future.

That's how we have gotten to this retirement crisis. People are just nervous. They worry, "Am I going to have enough money?" They can't count on the stock market to give them the returns that they were expecting, they can't count on the banks to give them the returns that they were expecting, and they can't count on their employers to help supplement their retirement income.

The retirees I talk to have reasonable goals. The most common thing I hear from retirees is, "I just want to be able to maintain the standard of living that I had when I was working." They want to be able to travel a little bit more than they used to. They want to be able to enjoy time with their children and with their grandchildren. They want to be able to possibly help fund their grandchildren's education. They basically want to spend time with family and enjoy the things that they like, without having to sacrifice the lifestyle they are used to.

THE RETIREMENT-NEEDS RULE OF THUMB

To have that lifestyle we all want in retirement, you have to ask yourself some key questions. Basically, the rule of thumb to continue to be able to fund your pre-retirement lifestyle is that you need to have about 80 percent of your pre-retirement income. So if you were earning $100,000 a year while you were working, you should be able to maintain that same lifestyle on about $80,000 a year. The reason you can survive on 20 percent less is because there are a lot of expenses associated with working that aren't going to be there anymore—things like clothing or uniforms. You don't spend money on lunch with coworkers, and you don't have to pay for gas and other commuting costs. There is a little drop in your income needs when you retire, but it's not a huge drop. Therefore, you need to remember the rule of thumb for retirees. Plan on having about 80 percent of your working income available to you during retirement, in order to maintain the lifestyle that you've become accustomed to. That should be your goal as you plan for your retirement.

So once you know your goal, you need to start taking steps to plan for your retirement. The first thing you should do is meet with a professional retirement advisor. This is complicated stuff, and if you don't spend time building your plan, you could end up unnecessarily costing yourself a lot of money.

WHY YOU NEED A RETIREMENT SPECIALIST

A lot of retirees might be working with someone at their local bank branch or even someone at their local stock firm. Maybe they are working with someone from their insurance company, because those firms are doing retirement planning now as well. The problem is that they are generalists. That means that they sit down with clients throughout the day with all sorts of different needs—a 22-year-old kid just out of college who wants to start saving for retirement; a married couple who has just had their first child and want to start saving not only for their retirement but also for their child's college fund; people in their 40s who have to really start paying for tuition because their children are in college; and people in their 60s who are in retirement. You will be much better served by finding a retirement specialist; someone who spends all of his or her time working with individuals who are retired or who are near retirement. Specialists work with people just like yourself every day and will do a better job putting together a plan for you as compared to a generalist.

NO CRYSTAL BALLS

Are you currently working with another financial advisor? Let me ask you: Does your financial advisor have a crystal ball that actually works? It's been my experience that almost every financial advisor says two things: 1.) They ask where your money is now; and 2.) They say, "Give your money to me because I can do a better job managing it." The problem is that they don't have a crystal ball. Well, guess what? No one does.

In my opinion, financial advisors are basically historians. They'll take a look at what the stock market has done in the past. Then they try to make an educated guess based on that information to predict where the stock markets will be going. But they don't have all the answers to make that kind of statement. Beware of anybody who says he or she can predict the market. Nobody can, and in our profession we're not allowed to make forward-looking statements based on past performance.

During your working years, the fluctuations of the stock market are not a big deal. Retirees have different needs than working people, and those different needs affect your investing strategy. The key difference is that when you're working, the fluctuations of the stock market really don't affect your lifestyle that much. Sure, you get your 401(k) statement and if you see that it's down it will cause you concern, but it doesn't cause you to change your lifestyle. When you're working, it is your paycheck that actually puts food on your table, gas in your car, and clothes on your back. That paycheck is the income that's coming in every week or every two weeks from your employer. That is what is dictating your lifestyle. Your lifestyle is not determined by your 401(k) balance or your stock portfolio balance. Your paycheck is the thing that determines how you live, where you live, what you buy, and how much you travel.

When you are retired and you no longer have that paycheck coming in every week, you rarely hear someone tell you to stop investing for growth and to start investing with a mind-set toward preservation. So most people are still trying to grow their money. When you're still trying to grow your money as a retiree, you are in a situation loaded with danger. When you are retired and depending on your retirement assets, rather than your paycheck, the fluctuations of the stock market do have a big effect on your lifestyle.

Too often retirees stay in this paycheck mode long after they've stopped collecting a paycheck. Their financial advisors are sometimes complicit in this. Maybe your advisor has not said, "Now that you're not working anymore, let's protect your money, let's preserve." Instead, the advisor is still trying to grow your money. And you know what you get when you try to grow your money? That's right, RISK should be limited as much as possible in your retirement.

Professional retirement specialists design retirement income plans. That's what they focus on, much more than growing your money. Sure, a professional retirement specialist will still grow your money, but his or her primary focus is protecting it. That's why you need a retirement specialist who understands that preservation and risk avoidance are important for retirees.

KEEPING UP WITH INFLATION

The true financial plan for retirement is never finished because your needs are always going to change. Let's say you're retiring at age 60 and you have a plan in place to generate $1,000 a month of income, based on what your needs are today. That might be great for the first two, three or four years of retirement. But things are always changing in your life personally, and things are always changing in the economy and in the world. A big factor regarding those changes is inflation. Just because you need $1,000 a month today in 2012, that $1,000 a month is not going to go as far in 2015, because of inflation. You need to regularly revisit your plan for that reason. You need to create a plan that will run the course and continue to increase your income to keep up with inflation.

Once you've made sure that your plan will be able to increase income to keep pace with inflation, then you want to identify your specific needs. Look at what has changed in the last year, since you first put the plan in place. Maybe there's a new grandchild in the picture and you want to start putting a little money away in a college fund. That's a new expense and planning factor that you didn't have three years ago. Things are always changing in everybody's lives. You want to keep revisiting your retirement plan to make sure that your plan is always working for you based on what your needs are today, not what those needs were three or five years ago.

THE ULTIMATE GOAL OF YOUR RETIREMENT PLAN

Where is your personal finish line? What is one of the biggest fears today? Is it dying too soon or is it living too long? Based on my 20 years of experience helping retirees, I have to say that people today are more worried about living too long and running out of money than dying too soon. When you look at how life-expectancy rates have risen over the past century, that concern makes a lot of sense. In the old days, many people would retire at age 65 and then die at age 66. When that was the case, we wouldn't need much of a retirement plan, would we? But now that people are living longer and longer, their biggest fear isn't dying too soon, it's living too long and running out of money.

You need to have a plan that guarantees that no matter how long you and your spouse live, you will never run out of money. In other words, you need to know that you will always reach your finish line no matter where it is. The basic financial goal of any retiree is a retirement plan that guarantees a stream of income that won't run out no matter how long you need it. That's what you need to really enjoy a worry-free retirement. The goal of this book is to help you create that retirement plan.

Risk, Income and Taxes

Chapter Two

When you start planning for your retirement, I want you to focus on three areas: 1) reducing risk; 2) increasing income; and 3) lowering taxes and fees.

RISKY BUSINESS: A CAUTIONARY TALE

Let me tell you about someone I talked to recently. He and his wife retired in 2004. At the time, he was 54 years old and she was 51 years old. They had $1,000,000 for their retirement. In 2004, he told his advisor, "I need $45,000 a year or about $3,700 a month." And the advisor told him, "Well, that's only 4.5 percent. That's easy to do. You'll be set for the rest of your life."

So his advisor had him keep 100 percent of his money in the stock market. Well, here we are eight years later, and his $1,000,000 is now worth $500,000. He lost half the value in eight years. He's only 62 years old now and he's on track to run out of money in the next seven to ten years when he and his wife are still going to be a relatively young couple. If his plan had been set up in guaranteed accounts where he had $45,000 guaranteed for the rest of his life, he'd be sitting pretty, but right now, he's scared to death about either running out of money or having to reduce his income substantially. One or the other is going to happen. It's simple math, and it's too late now to go back and correct the mistakes that were made eight years ago.

His problem was pretty simple; he had 100 percent of his money in the stock market during a period when the stock market was performing very poorly. From 2004 to 2011, the stock market experienced a lot of volatility, so his portfolio went from $1,000,000 to $500,000—a nightmare scenario for anyone. That's the danger of having too much risk in your portfolio when you're retired. If he were 34 years old, having his portfolio fluctuate up and down would not be a big deal to him because he wouldn't be depending on that portfolio for income. Now that he's retired, you can clearly see where having too much risk in his account has basically devastated his retirement.

Risk also threatens your ability to increase income. In this case, he has no ability to increase his income. In fact, he might have to decrease his income because of the substantial risks he has taken. Risk and income work hand in hand. If you're taking on too much risk, then you run the very real chance that you're going to have to decrease your income over the years, when you should be increasing it because of inflation.

Also, this man I spoke with was in a managed stock account, which means some of the losses he incurred were due to management fees. His brokers were taking a 1.5 percent fee, year in and year out, from his account. Even though he was losing money on his account, the stock company that he was working with was still making 1.5 percent on his assets. Granted, the fee was going down as the portfolio was going down, but the stock company was still putting money in its pocket while his assets were decreasing.

Sounds pretty bad, right? And we haven't even considered the effect of taxes on his losses. He was taking out $45,000 a year of income, and he was paying taxes on that $45,000 a year. His portfolio could have been structured in such a way that he was receiving $45,000 without having to pay taxes on the whole amount. It could have been set up in a more tax-efficient way so that he got the income he needed without having to pay as much in taxes.

This is why it's so important to pay attention to the risk, to pay attention to the taxes, and to pay attention to the fees, because all of that works hand in hand. It all affects how much income you're ultimately able to derive from your retirement assets. If the man in this story had a different plan, he could have addressed these factors from the very beginning, and he'd be in a much better place right now. If he had been working with a retirement specialist, he very well might still have had his $1,000,000. He could have been set up to receive his $45,000 per year with a guarantee for the rest of his life. He also could have possibly reduced the amount he paid in taxes over the years. Finally, he would have the ability to increase his income to cover inflation costs, which he would certainly need, because things cost more today than they did back in 2004.

THE 5 PERCENT PROBLEM

Think about all of the knowledge that's out there—on the Internet, in the libraries, and in the encyclopedias. Studies tell us that each individual knows about 5 percent of the knowledge out there, and that everybody's 5 percent is different. The 5 percent that I know is different than the 5 percent that you know. And it's different than the 5 percent your neighbor would know, and the 5 percent your lawyer would know. Everybody has his or her own 5 percent of knowledge based on life experiences.

Those same studies say that about 20 percent of the knowledge out there are things that we know we don't know. For example, I know there are lots of skill sets that I don't have. I know I can't speak a foreign language. I know I can't fly an airplane. I know I can't perform surgery. There are plenty of things that I know I have no expertise in or knowledge about. So that basically leaves 75 percent of knowledge out there that we don't even know we don't know.

When I talk to retirees and explain the different ways to get guaranteed income without taking market risk, or reducing taxes on all that income, they look at me kind of strangely and say, "Well, that doesn't exist." I explain to them that these ways are part of that 75 percent of the knowledge out there that people don't even know exists.

I'd like you to open up your mind to that 75 percent of knowledge, because in this book I'm going to share some new ideas about retirement planning with you, ideas I would guess you have never heard before.

THE THIRD WAY TO GET INCOME FROM YOUR ASSETS

Most people look at income from their assets as something they can get in one of two ways. They can either get it from what I call the "bank way" or they can get it the brokerage account way. If you're getting income the "bank way," that means you're basically putting your money into bank products such as CDs, and depending on what the banks are paying at the time, which dictates what your income is going to be. Let's imagine someone retiring today who has a million dollars. If he or she were relying on the bank to give them income, they'd be in trouble because bank CD rates are around 1 percent right now. That means this retiree is going to realize about $10,000 worth of income on that $1,000,000. That's not much. Imagine trying to replace a $50,000 or $60,000 salary with $10,000.

The other way to generate income is through what I call the "brokerage account way." That's when you put your money into stocks or bonds or mutual funds. Most stockbrokers will tell you that you can take 4 or 5 percent from that investment and you should be okay. But, again, remember my example of the retiree I talked to who was taking 4.5 percent from his investment, while the stock market was going down the whole time. He's in trouble right now. You want to look at ways that you can get as much income as you can while having that income guaranteed. And that's where insurance companies come in. Insurance companies are the outfits that have been the backbone of pension plans for all these big companies for the last 150 years. They are able to give you a guaranteed rate of return on your assets that most times is higher than what the bank is paying, and will be guaranteed income as opposed to what the brokerage houses are paying you. We'll talk more about how insurance company investments can help you create a guaranteed retirement income stream in Chapter Seven.

DON'T PAY TAXES YOU DON'T HAVE TO

Next, you need to understand how taxes can impact your retirement income. Let's stick with the example that you have a million dollars in a bank CD, and it's paying you 1 percent. That $10,000 is going to show up on your tax return as $10,000. Even if you weren't taking the income, even if you were reinvesting the income, that $10,000 is going to show up on your tax return as $10,000 of income. Fortunately, you can defer taxes or reduce taxes by using simple tax-reduction strategies.

Let's say you do need that income. So, we need to develop a plan that allows you to take that $10,000 of income from a source other than a bank CD, so you're taking it from a tax-efficient investment. Even though you're getting the same $10,000 in your pocket that the bank would give you, what is going to show up on your tax return may only be $1,000, rather than $10,000, because we're using tax-reduction strategies. We will talk a lot more about tax-reduction and tax-deferral strategies in Chapter Three.

DEATH BY A THOUSAND FEES

Almost every brokerage account out there has hard-dollar fees that are a percent of your assets. It might be 1 percent, 1.5 percent, or 2 percent per year. But these brokerage houses also have internal expenses that you don't even see. For mutual funds, the average fees are about 1.5 percent to 2 percent. On variable annuities they charge fees anywhere from 3 percent to 5 percent. You do not get a bill for these fees. It's not a hard line item on your statement. Those fees are buried in the back as internal expenses, but they do come out every year, and they do reduce your earnings.

So I'm sure you're saying, "Nobody likes to pay fees, but how can I avoid them when everybody charges them?" The answer goes back to that 75 percent of the knowledge you don't know you don't know.

One way to avoid these fees is to make sure you are not in an account where you're paying the broker or the brokerage house a hard-dollar fee. If you agree to something like that, you're stuck.

You're going to pay 1 percent or 1.5 percent or 2 percent of your assets year in and year out, no matter what the performance of the portfolio is. One way to avoid these fees is to just avoid any of those kind of managed accounts where they're going to be charging you a fee no matter what. Just say no.

Another way to avoid fees is to stay away from things like variable annuities or loaded mutual funds, where there are internal fees every year that you don't necessarily see, but they are disclosed to you at the beginning of the investment through the prospectus. Read any prospectus slowly and be on the lookout for red flags. Most people don't read the prospectus and aren't aware of those fees, but any investment that has a stock or a bond component to it, like a mutual fund or a variable annuity, is going to have fees of 2 to 4 percent. You want to avoid those kinds of investments.

You're not going to be able to avoid all fees. Everybody's going to charge you a fee—it's just the way of the world. You don't get something for nothing, but you do want to be cognizant of what those fees are. Because if you're paying 2 percent to 4 percent in fees and the return on your investment is only 5 percent, then half of your return is eaten up right there in the fees. They have a huge impact on your bottom line.

REDUCE YOUR RISK, OR ELSE

The simple way to reduce risk is to not put the dollars you need for retirement in the stock market. I'm not opposed to using the stock market for some of your growth; the stock market can be a fine way to grow your assets, but not at the risk of your retirement income. The key is to have your retirement needs met first with safe investments—not risky ones. Let's go back to my example again of the man who retired in 2004 with $1,000,000. He determined that he needed $45,000 per year in retirement. Well, that $1 million dollars should not have been anywhere near the stock market. Instead, he put the whole $1 million in the stock market. If he had avoided the market, he could have potentially had his $45,000 guaranteed for life. He would have been all set. If he had an additional $500,000, then, sure, he could take risks in the stock market with that extra money, if he was so inclined, because if that money fluctuated or went down, it wouldn't impact his retirement. Why would it be okay in this case? Because he would already have guaranteed his $45,000 per year with the million dollars. So the extra $500,000 is money he can afford to lose (I don't want to say it's play money because that trivializes it) without having an impact on his standard of living in his retirement.

THE RULE OF THUMB ON STOCK MARKET EXPOSURE (AND WHY IT'S WRONG)

There's a simple calculation people use to get a general idea of how much of their money should be in the stock market. The rule of thumb is that you subtract your age from 100 and that's the percentage of your money that should be in the stock market. So if you are 60 years old, then the rule of thumb says you should have no more than 40 percent of your money in the stock market.

Personally, I think this rule of thumb falls short for people who are getting close to retirement. My rule of thumb is that you shouldn't put any more money in the stock market than you can afford to lose without affecting your retirement income. So, again, if it takes 90 percent of your assets to guarantee your retirement income, then 90 percent of your assets had better stay out of the market. If it only takes 30 percent of your assets to guarantee your retirement income, then that's what stays out of the stock market. So the percent of your assets that should be in the stock market is an individual number. It's not a hard-and-fast rule. Take a look at your own situation to decide how much you can afford to risk in the stock market, and don't risk a penny more.

CHAPTER 3
The Three Phases of Retirement

Chapter Three

The one thing you need in retirement more than anything else is a change in mind-set. I know people who spend more time planning their vacations than they do planning their retirement. Basically, in your life you will have three phases that dictate how (and how much) you should think about your retirement. The first phase is the accumulation phase; the second phase is the preservation phase; and the third phase is the distribution phase.

THE ACCUMULATION PHASE

The accumulation phase basically starts when you enter the workforce—whatever age that is when you're done with college and you're starting to work. Hopefully, that's when you start saving for retirement. Those savings won't be a lot in the beginning, but it's something.

For a lot of people, the only foray into the accumulation stage as a young person is through their company's 401(k) plan. They don't start planning things on their own until a little bit later, but any time they're putting money away and have it in the back of their minds that the money they're saving is for your retirement, that's the accumulation phase. This is the phase when people can afford to take risks with their money. If someone is leaving college at age 22 or age 23 and not retiring until age 65, then he or she has a 40-to-45-year horizon in which to take risks. In this phase, you don't worry so much if the market's down for the first four or five years, because you still have another 30 years or so to make back any losses you incur. The accumulation phase starts in your early 20s and should go until age 45 to 55, depending on what your retirement goals are.

During the accumulation phase, you're probably putting 70 to 80 percent of your money in the stock market into things like large-cap stocks, small-cap stocks, bonds, partnerships and international investments. You're taking risks because that's where the potential for the greatest growth is. As you get closer to retirement, you want to transition some of your growth assets into the preservation phase because the closer to your retirement you get, the less time you're going to have to recover any stock market losses that come your way. If you plan to retire at age 65, you want to start transitioning from accumulating assets to preserving them 10 to 15 years before. This period is what I call the preservation phase.

THE PRESERVATION PHASE

Let's say you plan to retire at age 65. When you get to age 50 or age 55, you want to start transitioning into the preservation phase of your retirement saving. If you have 80 percent of your money in the stock market during the accumulation phase, then start reducing from 80 percent to 60 percent during those five years. When you're five to 10 years away from retirement, reduce those assets in the stock market from 60 percent to 40 percent. Then, from years five to one before retirement, reduce those assets again from 40 percent to 20 percent. The idea is to slowly reduce your exposure to the stock market because you're going to have less and less time to make up for any losses the closer they occur to your retirement. Think about the preservation phase as a slow, well-planned retrenchment from risky investments to safe investments.

This preservation time—10 to 15 years before retirement—is when you want to start talking to a professional retirement advisor, if not sooner. The people who come talk to me are anywhere from six months to 10 years away from retirement. That's really when you want to get serious about transitioning your assets from accumulation to preservation.

THE DISTRIBUTION PHASE

Once you are retired, you should have 90 to 100 percent of your money out of the market. Again, it depends on your individual situation and how much risk you can afford. As you slowly transition to the preservation phase, realize that you will stay in this phase for the rest of your life. Your primary goal is to preserve your money, not to try to grow it. The distribution phase is when you start taking money from your investments to supplement your retirement. This phase begins when you retire and start collecting Social Security or you start collecting your pension, if you're entitled to one. You start taking money from your assets to continue your pre-retirement lifestyle.

THE MOST COMMON MISTAKES PEOPLE MAKE

People make mistakes in all three of these phases, so make sure you avoid these errors. The No. 1 mistake I see in the accumulation phase is that *people aren't diversified enough in their assets.* They may have all of their assets in their company's stock, for example. Procter & Gamble is a huge employer where I live, in northeastern Pennsylvania. I see so many people who have 100 percent of their 401(k) in Procter & Gamble stock. That's great when Procter & Gamble stock is doing very well. People can make a ton of money in their 401(k) if they have all their money in one stock and the stock is doing well. But of course, the opposite can happen. If that one stock has a bad year, then 100 percent of their 401(k) is going to suffer. You can't afford to take that kind of risk. Lack of diversification is the single biggest mistake that I see in the accumulation phase.

In the preservation phase, the biggest mistake I see is that *people aren't conservative enough with their investments.* In some cases, they don't change their investments at all. I see many people who are 10, five or even one year away from retirement, and they still keep 80, 90, or even 100 percent of their money in the stock market when they should be moving those assets to safer investments.

When we look at the distribution phase, I see two main mistakes. The first is that *people take their money from a stock portfolio, instead of transitioning it to a safer place.* I've seen retirees lose as much as 40 percent of their retirement savings in the last decade, not because they were unlucky or uninformed, but because they were still operating in paycheck mode. The second mistake is that *people don't realize that there are tax-efficient ways to distribute their money.* They think the only way to get that distribution is just to take it out, and they are not mindful of the tax-reduction strategies that exist out there.

Below is a summary of the phases of retirement and what your investment strategy should be during each phase:

1. The Accumulation Phase (age 22-50)
   Paycheck mode, grow your retirement savings; you have time to recover from a loss in the stock market; be sure to diversify your portfolio.
2. The Preservation Phase (50-Retirement)
   Gradually change your goals from growing your assets to protecting them; talk to a professional retirement advisor; don't risk too many of your assets in the stock market.
3. The Distribution Phase (Retirement)
   Make sure you have moved the retirement-income-generating portion of your portfolio out of the stock market and withdraw your money as tax-efficiently as possible.

THE GOOD NEWS AND BAD NEWS ABOUT LIFE EXPECTANCY

Our life expectancy is higher than ever before and getting even higher. That's great news, but unfortunately our increased life expectancy is the cause of a lot of anxiety about retirement. According to a recent Gallup survey, 66 percent of retirees said their biggest fear is not that they're going to die any time soon, but that they are going to live too long and run out of money.

Evolution of Life Expectancy

Year 1900 - average life expectancy was 47

Year 1920 - average life expectancy was 54

Year 1940 - average life expectancy was 62

Year 1960 - average life expectancy was 69

Year 1980 - average life expectancy was 71

Year 2004 - average life expectancy was 80

People are living longer, medical science is better and people are taking better care of themselves.

SOURCE: NCHS- Mortality Data from the National Vital Statistics System, April 20th, 2005

That's an understandable fear when you look at how life expectancy has changed over the past 50 years. Think about someone who was retiring in the 1960s at age 65, when the average life expectancy was only 70. That's only a five-year retirement. When you're funding a five-year retirement, you're not really concerned about running out of money, because funding a five-year retirement isn't hard to do. But with people living longer and longer these days, someone who has reached age 65 has a better than 50 percent chance that they're going to live into their late 80s. That means you're looking at a 25-year retirement. That's where the risk of running out of money comes into play.

People need to be mindful of the fact that they're probably going to live longer than they think they are and they have to prepare for the worst. It's sounds funny when you say it like that. How can "the worst" be living longer? But you have to prepared to live to age 90 or even age 95 and make sure your retirement plan addresses that possibility.

Obviously, increased longevity affects the distribution phase of your retirement. This is where using insurance companies comes into play. You can set up retirement income accounts through insurance companies that will pay you a guaranteed income; no matter how long you live. So whether you live till age 85, 95, or 115, these funds are guaranteed to pay that income for the rest of your life. Other plans offered through banks or through the brokerage accounts pay out until the account is empty, but the insurance companies have to pay that income for as long as you're alive, even if your account value is zero.

RETIREES WANT MORE SAFETY, NOT MORE RISK

All the retirees I talk to say that they want more safety, not more risk. Like good marathon runners, they just want to be able to keep going and stay on their feet. Earlier in this chapter, I talked about how I see too many people with their entire portfolio invested with one company. Without question, the biggest mistake is a lack of diversification in investments. Diversification is an important topic, but the diversification you have during the accumulation phase is different than the diversification you're going to have in the preservation and distribution phases.

In the accumulation phase, your diversification is going to be stocks. In the stock realm there are many choices such as large-cap stocks, small-cap stocks and international stocks. There are also bonds and partnerships. There are so many different ways to diversify in the accumulation phase, but when you're in the preservation and the distribution phase there's really only one choice: Risk or safety?

A lot of times I meet retirees and they tell me, "Well, you know, I just have a little bit of risk." My response is always the same. I say, "Well, there's really no such thing as a little bit of risk." Your money is either at risk—which means it's someplace where you have the chance of losing it—or it's in a safer place. Every retiree I talk to says, "I want more safety, not more risk, with my investments." That's why in the preservation phase we should move your investments toward more and more safety with less and less risk.

This is precisely the change in mind-set that needs to take place as you move closer to retirement. For most people, if you ask them, "What does your retirement plan look like?" they're going to give you a blank stare and say, "I really don't have one. I get my Social Security check, I get my pension check, and, you know, that's it." If you press even further and ask, "What's your plan to guarantee that you're never going to run out of money no matter how long you live?" they'll say, "I don't have that. You know, I just hope I don't run out of money." Basically, their entire plan is hope.

Retirement can be the most rewarding period in your life, but living without that regular paycheck is a whole new ball game. Getting your money somewhere safe—without risk—where it can provide you and your spouse with a dependable stream of income is crucial.

CHAPTER 4
Tax Deferral Strategies

Chapter Four

How would you like to lower your taxes? When a professional retirement advisor starts to build your financial plan, the first thing to do is an evaluation of your tax return. If you are already working with a financial advisor, ask yourself if you are actively getting tax advice from him or her. Very often if you ask for tax advice, a financial advisor will tell you to ask your CPA or accountant, but most CPAs are not trained in giving financial advice. They'll look at your situation and tell you how much you owe based on what happened in the past, but many of them aren't able to tell you what to change in the present so you can lower your taxes in the future. Remember, it's not what you make, it's what you keep. Here's how you can keep more of your money through proper tax planning.

I'm not a CPA nor do I offer specific tax advice, but in this chapter I will offer you some general guidelines to consider as you consult with a tax expert.

What are the key tax-reduction strategies? First, use tax deferral. With tax deferral, you are taking advantage of what's called triple compounding. This is when you are making interest three ways: on your principal, on your interest, and on the taxes that you are not paying every year. Another way to reduce your taxes is to minimize your Social Security tax. Are you paying taxes on your Social Security? If you are, I am sure you don't like it. There may be ways to reduce or even eliminate those taxes on your Social Security income. Another way to reduce your tax bill is to generate tax-free or tax-favored income, and there are a lot of ways to do that. That's why I always encourage people to have their tax return evaluated to see if there are tax-reduction strategies that you can take advantage of and start keeping more of your money immediately.

DON'T FORGET TO INCLUDE TAXES WHEN CALCULATING YOUR RETURNS

When you're working with retirement-planning specialists, they are trained in financial-planning strategies that don't just look at reducing your tax bill this year, but reducing your tax bill long term. A retirement-planning specialist looks at what happened in the past and looks at things that could change today, to ensure that you're paying less in taxes tomorrow. Remember that man who retired with $1,000,000 in 2004? Let's say he invested that $1,000,000 in CDs. If I looked at his tax return and I saw $10,000 of interest income showing up on it, I would ask, "Where does this $10,000 come from?" He'd say, "It's from my million dollars in CDs." As a retirement-planning specialist, I immediately start looking at other strategies to get that $10,000, without having $10,000 showing up on that line on his tax return. Instead, I might try to develop a solution where he gets that same $10,000, but where only $1,000 or $2,000 shows up on the line in his tax return.

Again, it's not what you make; it's what you keep. Most people aren't thinking about the large effect taxes can have on their returns. They know the bank is paying 1 percent on a CD, and that's all they are focused on. They're not focused on what their bottom line is after taxes. For example, if you're making $10,000 in interest income on a CD, but you're in the 15 percent tax bracket, then you are actually only making $8,500 on that investment.

In this case, your actual rate of return is 0.85 percent after taxes. That's why you need to look at what the rate of return is after taxes are paid before you compare investment options. If someone is able to make 1 percent, and they're paying very little or no taxes on that money, then the absolute rate of return on that investment is 1 percent versus the absolute rate of return on the other investment of 0.85 percent. The bottom line is what you're actually keeping in your pocket after taxes, not what the top line entry is.

HOW TRIPLE COMPOUNDING WORKS

When we talk about ways to save money on taxes, there are lots of different approaches. One of the first and most obvious ways is just using tax deferral to save on taxes. Tax deferral is a very generic term. People have heard it, but a lot of times they don't understand the true impact of tax deferral because with tax deferral, you're taking advantage of triple compounding. What triple compounding means is that your principal is earning interest, your interest is earning interest, and the taxes that you aren't paying every year are earning interest as well. Instead of paying taxes, that money is going back into your investment.

Triple compounding is a very powerful strategy. Here is an example of money growing in a taxable account versus money growing in a tax-deferred, triple-compounding account.

$100,000 INVESTMENT FOR SOMEONE IN THE 15 PERCENT TAX BRACKET FOR 10 YEARS EARNING 5 PERCENT A YEAR

Taxable Account	Tax-Deferred Account
$100,000	$100,000
$104,250	$105,000
$108,681	$110,250
$113,300	$115,763
$118,115	$121,551
$123,135	$127,628
$128,368	$134,010
$133,824	$140,710
$139,512	$147,746
$145,441	$155,133
$151,622	$162,889
$158,064	$171,034

MINIMIZE YOUR SOCIAL SECURITY TAX

When you collect your Social Security income, depending on how much overall income you have, that Social Security income may be subject to income tax. When I look at a client's tax return, one of the first things I look for is whether Social Security is being taxed. If it is, then we can use tax-reduction strategies that will put extra income in that client's pocket, because we can reduce the amount of taxes paid on Social Security income. For example, let's say you're collecting $10,000 of Social Security income, but you're being taxed on 50 percent of it. So if $5,000 of your Social Security income is subject to tax, that's obviously a hit to your bottom line. If you can reduce that 50 percent of the income that's being taxed down to 20 percent, well, that's extra money in your pocket because less of your Social Security income is subject to tax. Reducing your Social Security income that is subject to taxes is a simple way to protect your assets and a good reason why you should talk to a professional retirement advisor. I'll be talking a lot more about how to minimize your Social Security tax in Chapter Eight.

GENERATE TAX-FREE AND TAX-FAVORED INCOME

The next thing we need to look at is how to generate tax-favored income. This goes back to our example of the retiree who's collecting $10,000 on that CD income. If all of that $10,000 is being taxed, we can look at strategies where maybe only $1,000 of that income is being taxed, or just $500 of that income is being taxed. We want to use the different tax strategies that are out there that allow us to save money on taxes. There are lots of ways to generate tax-free and tax-favored income. It really depends on people's specific situation what strategy is used to take advantage of that. In fact, I think it will be easier for you to understand this concept if I use a real-world example, a retired couple I work with named George and Shirley.

GEORGE AND SHIRLEY

A couple of years ago, I met George and Shirley at one of my retirement-planning workshops, and we started working together on their retirement plan. When George and Shirley came to me, they had about $600,000 in CDs that were paying, at the time, 5 percent. So they were generating $30,000 of income from the CDs. They had $200,000 in stocks, and the dividends on those stocks were $9,000. When they came to me, their biggest concern wasn't taxes. They were paying $7,300 in taxes on that $39,000 of income, but that wasn't a concern to them. Their main concern was, "Hey, these CDs are coming due now and the bank only wants to renew them at 2 percent, rather than 5 percent." This meant their income was going to drop from $30,000 down to $12,000. Understandably, George and Shirley were in a little bit of a panic. If the banks were only going to pay 2 percent on CDs, how could they keep their income as high as it used to be?

As part of my evaluation, I looked at their tax return and saw that of the almost $40,000 of income and dividends that they were receiving, they were paying tax on all of it. They were paying between $7,200 and $7,300. So, to help offset the effect of that lower interest rate on the CDs, I was able to reposition their $800,000 into tax-efficient investments. With that $800,000 in tax-efficient investments, I was able to generate $48,000 a year for them that would be guaranteed for the rest of both of their lives. Never again do they have to worry about CDs coming due and the rates going down.

We were also able to take advantage of what's called the exclusion ratio, which means they're getting $48,000 of income, but most of that $48,000 is excluded on the tax return. That first return I looked at had $39,000 of income and it all showed up on George and Shirley's tax return. But on the new tax return they're getting $48,000 of income, but only $8,000 shows up as income. The other $40,000 is excluded from the income. That's why it's called the exclusion ratio, because only $8,000 is taxed—$40,000 is excluded—and that lowers George and Shirley's total tax liability from $7,300 down to $653.

GEORGE AND SHIRLEY'S TAX RETURN, BEFORE AND AFTER

				Before	After
Income	7	Wages, salaries, tips, etc. Attach Form(s) W-2	7	9,778	9,778
	8a	**Taxable interest.** Attach Schedule B if required	8a	29,443	8,127
Attach Form(s) W-2 here. Also attach Forms W-2G and 1099-R if tax was withheld.	b	Tax-exempt interest. **Do not** include on line 8a [8b] 88			
	9a	Ordinary dividends. Attach Schedule B if required	9a	9,482	0
	b	Qualified dividends (see page 22) [9b] 3,637			
	10	Taxable refunds, credits, or offsets of state and local income taxes (see page 23)	10	614	614
	11	Alimony received	11		
	12	Business income or (loss). Attach Schedule C or C-EZ	12		
If you did not get a W-2, see page 22.	13	Capital gain or (loss). Attach Schedule D if required. If not required, check here ► ☐	13	-3,000	-3,000
	14	Other gains or (losses). Attach Form 4797	14		
	15a	IRA distributions [15a] b Taxable amount (see page 24)	15b	0	0
	16a	Pensions and annuities [16a] b Taxable amount (see page 25)	16b	12,689	3,856
Enclose, but do not attach, any payment. Also, please use Form 1040-V.	17	Rental real estate, royalties, partnerships, S corporations, trusts, etc. Attach Schedule E	17		
	18	Farm income or (loss). Attach Schedule F	18		
	19	Unemployment compensation in excess of $2,400 per recipient (see page 27)	19		
	20a	Social security benefits [20a] b Taxable amount (see page 27)	20b		
	21	Other income. List type and amount (see page 29)	21	6,000	0
	22	Add the amounts in the far right column for lines 7 through 21. This is your **total income** ►	22	64,926	19,375
Adjusted Gross Income	23	Educator expenses (see page 29) [23]			
	24	Certain business expenses of reservists, performing artists, and fee-basis government officials. Attach Form 2106 or 2106-EZ [24]			
	25	Health savings account deduction. Attach Form 8889 [25]			
	26	Moving expenses. Attach Form 3903 [26]			
	27	One-half of self-employment tax. Attach Schedule SE [27]			
	28	Self-employed SEP, SIMPLE, and qualified plans [28]			
	29	Self-employed health insurance deduction (see page 30) [29]			
	30	Penalty on early withdrawal of savings [30]			
	31a	Alimony paid b Recipient's SSN ► [31a]			
	32	IRA deduction (see page 31) [32] 6,000			
	33	Student loan interest deduction (see page 34) [33]			
	34	Tuition and fees deduction. Attach Form 8917 [34]			
	35	Domestic production activities deduction. Attach Form 8903 [35]			
	36	Add lines 23 through 31a and 32 through 35	36	6,000	0
	37	Subtract line 36 from line 22. This is your **adjusted gross income** ►	37	58,926	19,375

For Disclosure, Privacy Act, and Paperwork Reduction Act Notice, see page 97. Cat. No. 11320B   Form **1040** (2008)   Form **1040**

				Before	After
Tax and Credits	38	Amount from line 37 (adjusted gross income)	38	58,926	19,375
	39a	Check { ☐ **You** were born before January 2, 1945, ☐ **Blind.** } Total boxes { ☐ **Spouse** was born before January 2, 1945, ☐ **Blind.** } checked ► 39a			
Standard Deduction for—	b	If your spouse itemizes on a separate return or you were a dual-status alien, see page 35 and check here ► 39b ☐			
• People who check any box on line 39a, 39b, or 40b or who can be claimed as a dependent, see page 35.	40a	**Itemized deductions** (from Schedule A) **or your standard deduction** (see left margin)	40a	9,222	9,222
	b	If you are increasing your standard deduction by certain real estate taxes, new motor vehicle taxes, or a net disaster loss, attach Schedule L and check here (see page 35) ► 40b ☐			
	41	Subtract line 40a from line 38	41	49,704	10,153
• All others:	42	**Exemptions.** If line 38 is $125,100 or less and you did not provide housing to a Midwestern displaced individual, multiply $3,650 by the number on line 6d. Otherwise, see page 37	42	3,650	3,650
Single or Married filing separately, $5,700	43	**Taxable income.** Subtract line 42 from line 41. If line 42 is more than line 41, enter -0-	43	46,054	6,503
Married filing jointly or Qualifying widow(er), $11,400	44	Tax (see page 37). Check if any tax is from: a ☐ Form(s) 8814 b ☐ Form 4972	44	7,340	653
	45	**Alternative minimum tax** (see page 40). Attach Form 6251	45		
Head of household, $8,350	46	Add lines 44 and 45 ►	46	7,340	653
	47	Foreign tax credit. Attach Form 1116 if required [47]			
	48	Credit for child and dependent care expenses. Attach Form 2441 [48]			
	49	Education credits from Form 8863, line 29 [49]			
	50	Retirement savings contributions credit. Attach Form 8880 [50]			
	51	Child tax credit (see page 42) [51]			
	52	Credits from Form: a ☐ 8396 b ☐ 8839 c ☐ 5695 [52]			
	53	Other credits from Form: a ☐ 3800 b ☐ 8801 c ☐ [53]			
	54	Add lines 47 through 53. These are your **total credits**	54		
	55	Subtract line 54 from line 46. If line 54 is more than line 46, enter -0- ►	55	7,340	653
Other Taxes	56	Self-employment tax. Attach Schedule SE	56		
	57	Unreported social security and Medicare tax from Form: a ☐ 4137 b ☐ 8919	57		
	58	Additional tax on IRAs, other qualified retirement plans, etc. Attach Form 5329 if required	58		
	59	Additional taxes: a ☐ AEIC payments b ☐ Household employment taxes. Attach Schedule H	59		
	60	Add lines 56 through 59. This is your **total tax** ►	60	7,340	653

In this example, I not only lowered George and Shirley's taxes, but I also increased what they were earning. You're probably thinking that this seems too good to be true, but this type of tax-reduction planning is not uncommon. I increased George and Shirley's income by $9,000, which is now guaranteed for life, and then I saved them $6,600 in taxes. I talk about George and Shirley because they are such a great example of how getting professional retirement-planning advice can change your life for the better. They had $800,000 of assets, and they're receiving $48,000 per year of income. That comes to a 6 percent cash flow, and that 6 percent cash flow is going to be guaranteed for as long as both live. Imagine going down to your local bank and saying, "I'm going to give you this money for a CD and I want you to give me 6 percent interest income on it, and then when I die, I want to make sure my wife still continues to get that 6 percent interest income. And oh, by the way, I don't want to pay tax on all of that. I only want to pay taxes on a fraction of that income."

That bank is going to tell you to hit the road, but these types of investments are out there. This all goes back to that 75 percent of the knowledge that you don't even know exists. Investment strategies to increase and guarantee your retirement income are out there. You just have to know where to find them.

CHAPTER 5

The Stock Market Exit Plan

Chapter Five

By now, you understand that one of my bedrock principles of retirement planning is that as you get closer to retirement, you need to reduce, or in some cases eliminate, market risk.

KNOW YOUR "ENOUGH IS ENOUGH" NUMBER

When I present my anti-market risk approach to my new clients, a lot of times they agree with me in theory, but they say, "I don't want to do anything now because my accounts are so low," or "I want to wait until the stock market comes back a little bit. I want to recover." You know this reasoning. And I agree with it to a certain extent. A lot of times people have a dollar figure in mind that they'd like to get back to. Say they started with $100,000 and now it's worth $80,000. They're thinking, "If it gets back to $100,000 or even close to that, then I'll sell. I just don't want to sell at $80,000 right now." What I always tell these individuals is that even though they have a number on the upside where they feel they'll be comfortable selling, it's equally important, or maybe even more important, to have a number on the downside where they say, "Enough is enough."

Staying with that same example, if someone has $80,000 in their account and they started with $100,000, they should have a number in mind where they'll cut their losses and sell, no matter what. For example, maybe they decide that if it gets to $70,000, they'll say, "No matter what, we're getting out now." I always tell people, "If you don't have an exit strategy in mind, two years from now, you could be sitting here with an account worth $20,000." Then they're scratching their heads saying, "How the heck did I watch the account go from $100,000 to $20,000? How could I have been so stupid not to do anything?" The reason is because there was no defined exit strategy in the first place. They just kept watching their investment fall and fall and fall, without ever having a fixed number where "enough is enough." It's so important for people to have a number in mind on both the upside and the downside where they're going to exit the market. Having a number helps take the emotion out of it as well. The emotional side of investing is real. It's something you have to take into account. You need to take steps to limit the effect of your emotions on your financial decision-making.

If you don't have an exit plan, and you're just sitting there waiting for the account to get back to where it was, and that's the only parameter you have in mind, you could get in a lot of trouble. So again, let's say you started with $100,000 and now it's worth $80,000 and you're thinking, "I don't want to do anything until it gets back to even." Let's say you had invested in Lucent stock or General Motors stock. General Motors stock is a recent example of a stock that pretty much became worthless. What would have happened back in 2005, 2006 or 2007—before all the bailouts and the restructuring happened in the auto industry—if someone was holding onto

General Motors stock and waiting for it to come back without any exit plan? They would be sitting with that old General Motors stock, basically worthless, and getting no money back. Wouldn't you rather have had your $80,000 than nothing back? That's the danger of not having an exit plan on the downside. Yes, it's an extreme example, but it illustrates a point about risk; your money is either at risk or it's not. It's a worst-case scenario, but stocks can go to zero. If you're still holding those shares, then 100 percent of your money is lost, as opposed to only 20 percent if you sold back when the stock was worth $80,000.

In the sour economy of recent years, I have increasingly heard from retirees that they want to stay in the market to get at least some of their money back. When I explain my philosophy of keeping money safe, inevitably someone will say, "Yep. I want to do it, but I'm just going to hold on a little bit longer. I'm going to wait for the market to come back just a little bit." That's when I get up on my trusty soapbox and say, "That's all well and good, but you have to have a number in mind on the downside. If it crosses that number, come hell or high water, you're getting out."

BE LOGICAL, NOT EMOTIONAL

I don't want to sound heartless because I understand that losing money in the stock market causes an emotional response. People are emotional about their money and no one likes to admit making a mistake or admitting a failure. I know I don't like admitting failure. And when people sell at a loss, they're basically admitting a failure, and they don't want to do that. That's why they would much rather hold on to a stock and wait for it to come back to even before they sell, because then they don't have to say to themselves that the decision was a bad one.

That's why I want you to put a number on the downside. It takes the emotion out of the equation and replaces it with just an arbitrary objective number. It's math now that's dictating your decision, rather than emotion.

The funny thing is that even though people agree with the strategy of putting a number on it, probably half of them still don't do it. They still hold on to that stock and wait for it to come back and they sometimes get caught, almost paralyzed, watching this free fall. Everybody agrees with me, saying, "Oh yeah. I'll pick a number and sell when it gets there, no matter what. Okay." That's what they tell me they're going to do, but still half of the people don't follow that advice. It reminds me of gamblers down at the casino who keep pulling money out of their wallet trying to win back their losses. At the end of the day, you have to have a number where you cut your losses and quit.

THE "HEDGE" STRATEGY

In my practice, I never make stock recommendations about getting in the market. My advice is always about getting out of the market because I don't like market risk in retirement planning, and I especially hate risking money you can't afford to lose. My stock market advice boils down to two main points. The first one is the importance of having a number on the downside. The other one is the usefulness of a hedge when you want to wait for a stock to regain its value.

Many of the retirees I meet in northeastern Pennsylvania worked for Proctor & Gamble, and they still own Proctor & Gamble stock. I often hear from these retirees the same reasoning. "I want to wait till Procter & Gamble gets back to, you know, $80 a share and then I'll sell it. I want to wait till it gets back a little bit." After telling them to have a number on the downside, I suggest they hedge their bets by selling half their position in the stock. Let's say they sell half their stock at $60 a share. That way, if the stock market goes up, they're not kicking themselves saying, "Oh, geez. I sold all the shares. I have nothing. I should have held out to where I could have been making money." But, on the other side, if they sold half of their shares and the stock's still going down, they can say, "Yeah, okay. Well at least now I sold half of it and I don't have all my money in there now." When in doubt, that philosophy of hedging and selling half of your position is a good way to protect yourself.

I only use that hedge in situations when someone has a large position in a particular stock, rather than a collection of mutual funds or stocks. Even with the hedge, the most important thing is to make a commitment that if the portfolio hits a certain dollar amount, you know you have to get out no matter what.

HOW MUCH RISK CAN YOU AFFORD?

Everybody knows the stock market goes up and the stock market goes down. At least in theory, everybody is okay with the fluctuations of the stock market because people generally say, "Well, I don't need the money right now and it's only a paper loss if it goes down." That's true when you're investing as a 20-year-old or a 30-year-old for retirement because you're looking at a 30- to 40-year time horizon, and you can tolerate the ups and downs of the stock market when your retirement is so far off in the future. If you lose half of your portfolio in your 30s it doesn't feel good, but you can tell yourself, "Well, I don't need this money for 30 years. There's plenty of time for the stock market to come back and for me to recover my losses." But if that same situation happens when you're 55 years old, then you're only looking at a five-year period for the market to recover those losses. Obviously, it's much more difficult for a 50 percent loss to be recovered over a five-year period than over a 30-year period. That's why you want to have less and less exposure to the market as you get closer and closer to your retirement date.

Now understand that I'm not saying you shouldn't have any money in the stock market. Take a look at what your income needs are and make sure you factor in inflation, and then you can see how much income you require for your retirement. Once that need is met, you can look to the stock market to increase your income with the money you have left over. Let's say your income needs are $3,000 a month, and you can see that income need going up to $4,500 a month over the course of the next 20 to 30 years because of inflation. You want to set aside enough money in a fixed guaranteed account that will guarantee $3,000 a month of income for the first few years and slowly increase to keep up with inflation. In your retirement plan, you want to have enough money set aside so that – no matter how long you live—you're going to have enough money to account for your needs and for inflation.

Let's say that number is $400,000. If you need $400,000 to guarantee you'll have $3,000 a month now and factor in an increase for inflation, and you have a portfolio of $600,000, then the $400,000 has to be in a fixed account. You can't have that $400,000 associated with any risk. The other $200,000 can go into the stock market or any other risky accounts. If that $200,000 goes to zero it's not going to impact your lifestyle, because you'll have your income guaranteed on the other side.

CALCULATE YOUR INCOME NEEDS

Let's say you have calculated your income needs and you've determined that you have too much of your money at risk in the market. What happens next? The first thing you should do is sit down with a retirement income specialist and remove from the stock market the amount of money that you need to guarantee your income for life. Take that example we were just taking about. If someone came to me and said that he had $600,000 and it's all in the stock market, the first thing we would do is calculate the amount needed each month to fund his retirement. We do the calculations and determine that he needs to set aside $400,000 to guarantee that he will have sufficient income no matter how long he lives. Then my advice would be to reduce the stock portfolio from $600,000 down to $200,000 immediately and put that $400,000 into a safe vehicle, so he can guarantee his retirement income forever.

THE 401(K) TAX TIME BOMB

Let's talk about the biggest paycheck that most people will ever get from their employer. It's your IRA or 401(k) retirement plan. These retirement savings accounts could be the greatest benefit to you and your family, but they could also be the biggest tax time bomb. Properly titled beneficiary designations can double, triple, or even quadruple the value of your IRA or 401(k) to you and your beneficiaries. By contrast, improperly titled designations can cost you up to 60 percent of the value in taxes and penalties.

One of the most important things to understand about your 401(k) or IRA is the beneficiary designation and how important it is to do this correctly. For example, let's say a man has his wife listed as the primary beneficiary. When the husband passes away, 100 percent of that IRA will go to his wife. Basically, the IRA will now be titled in the wife's name, and she'll continue to enjoy that tax-deferred growth for as long as she's alive.

Where the problem potentially comes in is how the contingent beneficiaries are named, or not named. If children are named as contingent beneficiaries, what then happens is if the wife dies and the parents wanted the IRA to go 50-50 to the children, each one would have the ability to have their portion titled into an IRA in his or her name. They could continue that tax deferral for the course of their lifetimes as well, if they want it. They could also take a distribution, which would cause taxes and penalties and is not the optimal decision. They do have the option to continue with it in an IRA and continue the tax deferral.

If no contingent beneficiaries are named, then the money is paid out to the estate. Once the estate has gone through, we find out the IRA is supposed to go to the two children. The money is paid from the estate to the children 50-50, but when they get it, they're going to have to pay tax on that money automatically. They don't have the ability or the choice at that time to continue it as an IRA in their name. That's why it's important to have a contingent beneficiary named, so they can continue the tax deferral. If there's no contingent beneficiary named on your IRA, then your children are going to have to pay taxes on it when they eventually get the money.

What's more, that tax rate can be especially high; depending on which tax bracket they are in, as high as 50 percent or (gulp!) even higher. If they're taking that money, then it's taxed rather than tax-deferred. Number one, if they're under age 59-and-a-half, they're going to pay a pre-59-and-a half tax penalty that's levied by the IRS. Number two, the money they're receiving is going to be taxed at their ordinary tax bracket, whatever that is. If it's significant money, it could throw them into a much higher tax bracket. If they're in the 15 percent tax bracket normally, and they inherit an extra $200,000, that could kick them all the way up to the top tax bracket, which is 38 or 39 percent. Couple that with the 10 percent penalty on top, and we're getting close to 50 percent of the value gone in taxes and penalties.

That's a huge tax hit and one that is totally unnecessary, but people don't realize the importance of naming contingent beneficiaries. Almost everybody I see has the spouse named as primary beneficiary on their IRA. In 99 percent of the cases, there's a primary beneficiary named. I would venture to guess that probably 50 percent of the individuals I talk to don't have contingents named on their 401(k) or IRA accounts. They just assume it'll eventually work itself out and the money will get to their children. In one sense, they're correct. Eventually the money will trickle down to them. The problem is that if it trickles down to them the wrong way, those kids are going to be heavily taxed on it versus having that money trickle down the right way, where all that income is tax-deferred to them.

Fixed Income From A Fixed Portfolio

Chapter Six

Are you willing to have an income stream that fluctuates each month? Probably not. Your bills don't fluctuate each month. The amount of food and gas you need and your other expenses don't fluctuate much either.

FLUCTUATING INCOME=CONSTANT RISK

When I talk to retirees, one of the first things I ask is, "How many people are willing to have an income stream that goes up and down every month?" As you can imagine, nobody raises a hand. Then I say, "Okay, everybody wants a guaranteed or a fixed amount of income coming in monthly during retirement, much the same as when you were working." The paycheck is a model of income distribution that everybody understands. You had that fixed paycheck coming in. You could count on it. When you're in retirement, you still want that fixed payment coming in, something you can count on. Everybody agrees with that.

If you want a guaranteed or fixed amount of income coming in every month of your retirement, then you have to avoid the danger of taking a fixed amount of income from a fluctuating portfolio. When we talk about a fluctuating portfolio, we're looking at the stock market. When your retirement money is in the stock market, there are two things that can happen. If you're taking income from a fluctuating portfolio, either the amount of income you take will go up and down every month or, if you want to take a fixed amount, then your principal will go up and down every month. The danger with that scenario is that if you're taking a fixed amount of income from the stock market and the stock market is moving in the wrong direction (trending down), then the danger is very real that eventually you're going to run out of money.

THE "WORST THAT CAN HAPPEN" CAN HAPPEN

A very extreme example of a stock market moving in the wrong direction would be back in 1973, when the market was down about 50 percent in a year's time. If someone had put $100,000 in the stock market at the beginning of 1973, the account would have been worth about $55,000 just 18 months later.

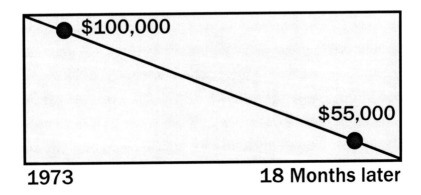

In 18 months, you've basically lost half of your money. Even if you weren't taking anything out of your principal, if you weren't taking any income, it would have taken you 13 years to get back to even. You wouldn't be back to $100,000 in the account until 1987.

I realize that past performance is not indicative of future performance, but how many people can afford to put their money into an investment and wait 13 years to get back to even? That's assuming you aren't taking any income from that investment. If you're taking a fixed amount in income from the portfolio, the picture gets even worse. Can you imagine if you were relying on this money for retirement and you had been pulling a monthly check? You would never be able to make it up. Depending on how much income you were taking, the account would have been depleted in five to 10 years.

The reason I give this example is because it's an eye-opener. It's not a make-believe, worst-case scenario. This actually happened. It doesn't mean that it will happen again, but the possibility is out there.

Then I ask, if that does happen again, how many people are willing to wait 13 years? Of course, nobody is willing to wait 13 years to get back to even. They can't afford to. This concept isn't just from the 1970s. Remember our example from earlier when I talked about the retiree who had a million dollars back in 2004 and was taking $45,000 a year from his account. The market has been down a lot since that time, and he had $500,000 just eight short years later. That's why it's so important to have a fixed, predictable income stream coming from a fixed portfolio rather than a fluctuating portfolio. When your income is coming from a fixed portfolio, you never have to worry about that account ever going to zero. That income will be guaranteed for life.

RISK ISN'T WORTH IT

When I talk to individuals who have money in the stock market, I always ask, "How many people would see a big change in their lifestyle if their account was up 30 percent over the next year or so?" Let's say you started with $500,000 and within 18 months it grew to $650,000. How many people will radically change their lifestyle? Would you go out and buy a Bentley? Or will you start jet-setting across to Europe a couple of times a year? People giggle and say no. That 30 percent increase is not going to change their lifestyle radically. It's not as if they won the lottery. If they won the lottery, then maybe they'd go out and start spoiling themselves, buying luxury cars and going on exotic vacations, but a 30 percent gain in their portfolio is not going to change their lifestyle.

So then I flip it and ask, "How many of you would see a big change in your lifestyle if you realized a 30 percent loss in your portfolio over the next year to 18 months?" You had $500,000, and here we are 18 months later, and it's worth $350,000. How many people are going to lose more than a couple nights' sleep worrying about that? And everybody raises a hand, because that's something that's going to bother them.

For the most part, losing 30 percent of their portfolio makes people change their lifestyle because they feel poor. That "poor" feeling even applies to people who are not taking income from their portfolio. Say someone doesn't have to rely on their assets for income. They have a pension and they have Social Security and those two income sources are enough to provide the lifestyle that they need. Even those who don't need to rely on their portfolio for income start cutting back after losses. Not because they don't feel rich, because I don't believe anybody ever feels rich, but because they don't feel that they have as much of a cushion as they used to have. If a couple have $500,000 sitting in their portfolio, they say, "Okay. we could spoil the grandkids a little bit. We could take that extra trip. We could do a little bit of the extras that maybe we would hesitate to do in poorer times." Then, if they wake up a year later, and their account is worth $350,000 rather than $500,000, they are certainly going to start cutting back on the extras. That's not just retirees, that's everybody. We see that a lot today. It's a Catch-22. All the experts say that people aren't going to start spending again and stimulate the economy until consumer confidence comes back and the market comes back. Then those same experts say the market is not going to come back and confidence isn't going to come back until people start spending money again. It's a vicious cycle. For one thing to happen, the other thing has to happen, so what really happens is nothing. People aren't spending because there's low confidence and the market stinks, but the market stinks because people aren't spending. How does that cycle end? Nobody knows.

The key question is, "If a 30 percent gain is not going to change your lifestyle significantly, but a 30 percent decrease is going to cause you anxiety, why are you bothering taking the risk in the first place?" No one has been able to give me a logical answer to that question. Everyone I talk to says that a 30 percent increase in income would not change his lifestyle, but that a 30 percent decrease would, so really, why take the risk?

I think it goes back to the fact that there are a lot of financial advisors out there who are offering only the stock-market option. Most advisors are not giving people any other options to look at to fund their retirement, so people assume that the stock market is the only way to go. They just accept that to grow your money, you have to take risks. It just goes with the territory. The truth is just the opposite. You don't need to take unnecessary risks with your retirement money, and if you need that money to fund your lifestyle, then you absolutely should not take risk. (Be boring with your money.) The stock market is fine for some of your money if you are looking for growth potential, but only after your income needs are satisfied first.

BORING WINS

Take a look at this chart of stock market gains and losses. I think most people would agree that it's a pretty typical decade of stock market returns—seven positive years and three negative years. It's up, it's down, but it's up more years than down in a good 10-year cycle.

I want you to think about these returns versus an investment that gave you consistent returns of 5 percent per year. I know— bo-ring!—but humor me.

Year	A	B
1	+15%	+5%
2	+16%	+5%
3	+10%	+5%
4	-17%	+5%
5	+10%	+5%
6	-5%	+5%
7	+16%	+5%
8	-8%	+5%
9	+10%	+5%
10	+6%	+5%

Which chart do you think gives the higher return? If you say Chart B, with the consistent 5 percent return, you're right. The boring 5 percent, 5 percent, 5 percent returns beat the wild ups and downs of the stock market by about $5,000 to $7,000 because just two or three down years can really throw your returns off.

$100,000 Lump Sum
Total A = $158,747
Total B = $162,889

Yup, boring wins. Most people don't realize how difficult it is to make up losses in the stock market. When the market goes down, a lot of people don't realize what you have to make the next year, just to get back to even. For example, if you lost 50 percent in the market one year, what do you think you need the next year to get back to even? Most people say, "Well, we need 50 percent to get back to even." That's wrong. The answer is you need 100 percent the next year to get back to even. If your account goes from $100,000 to $50,000, that's a 50 percent loss. If in the next year you want to go from $50,000 to $100,000, then you have to have a 100 percent gain, because a 50 percent gain is only going to get you back to $75,000, not to $100,000. It's just basic math. You need a higher return next year to make up for losses this year, which is why boring usually wins. Just two or three down years a lot of times underperforms getting a consistent and boring 5 percent a year, because of how hard it is to make up those losses.

So then the question is, "Where can I get 5 percent every year?" For the answer, turn the page to the next chapter.

CHAPTER 7

Opportunity Money and Safe Money

Chapter Seven

With CD rates at historic lows of 1 or 2 percent, people want to know where they can get those steady, dependable 5 percent returns. That's when I can see people's ears prick up. The truth is that there are two ways to invest your money. You can put your money in the world of safety, or you can put your money in the world of opportunity; that is, the world of risk.

WHAT IS SAFE MONEY?

When you look at the world of safety, there are really only three places where you can put money that it's going to be absolutely guaranteed without market risk. Those three places are the banks, the U.S. government through government bonds, or insurance companies with fixed annuities.

The world of safe money has pros and cons. The number one positive about the world of safe money is that your principal is going to be 100 percent guaranteed. No matter what happens, your principal is never going to be at risk. The second benefit of the world of safe money is that you could get a fixed income from that portfolio because it's guaranteed. With safe money, you can take a fixed amount of interest, whatever it's paying, and know that your principal is always going to be guaranteed. And then the third benefit, depending on how we set it up, is that there are some tax advantages that we could take a look at. Those tax advantages don't apply in all cases, but there is a chance that you could have some tax advantages in safe-money investments. That's something to look at very closely.

The downside of the world of safe money is that recently those investments have been offering very, very low returns. You're making close to 0 percent in savings accounts, and you're probably not making more than 2 percent in CDs. There's limited upside potential for safe money right now. You're stuck with low returns. There are also liquidity issues or penalties that might affect you. If you decide to sell a CD early, the bank will often hit you with some type of interest penalty. If you're cashing out a bond early, there are going to be interest penalties. If you're cashing out a fixed annuity early, there are surrender penalties. So, be aware that there are liquidity concerns with certain fixed income or guaranteed products.

THE PROS AND CONS OF SAFE MONEY

Pros:
1. Safety of Principal
2. Possible Tax Benefits
3. Fixed Income

Cons:
1. Early Redemption Fees
2. Low Returns
3. Limited Upside

WHAT IS OPPORTUNITY MONEY?

When we look at the world of opportunity, that's where you can make a decent amount of returns, potentially, with brokerage houses through stocks, bonds, mutual funds, and things like that. Or you could put your money with insurance companies through variable annuities. You're probably wondering how insurance companies can be listed under both safe money and opportunity money. The answer is that when we use insurance companies we're talking about using annuities. There are two types of annuities: a fixed annuity, where your principal is 100 percent guaranteed, and a variable annuity, where your principal is going to be at risk. A fixed annuity product would be considered safe money because the principal is guaranteed, where a variable annuity is opportunity money or risk money because your principal is at risk, and because you have the upside potential of the stock market.

Let's look at the pros and cons of putting your money in the world of opportunity. On the pro side, you really have unlimited upside potential. How many times have you heard stories of people doubling their money in a months' time or making a 200 percent return? The possibility exists to make a ton of money in the stock market. The downside of that is you also have the potential to lose 100 percent of your money. The good part of the opportunity is the upside potential. The downside is the risk that's involved. The other negative about opportunity money is that there are commissions and fees involved, so it costs you money to buy a stock or bond, or even to sell it. Whatever you do, there is going to be a fee involved. Very often, on stocks in particular, you're going to have to pay current taxes when you sell it. There's no tax deferral available with the stock market. When you sell a stock at a gain, you are going to pay taxes.

THE PROS AND CONS OF OPPORTUNITY MONEY

Pros:
1. Good Upside
2. Liquidity

Cons:
1. High Fees
2. Risk of Losses
3. Current Taxes

We have opportunity money on one side, where generally people hope to make between 10 and 12 percent a year. Not that you're going to make that, but if you're going to put your money at risk, the expectation is that you're going to make double-digit returns. On the other side, we have safe money, which currently is only making 1 or 2 percent. The reason people are so concerned right now is that they see no middle ground. Either they risk their money in a turbulent stock market, which has caused a lot of people pain in recent years, or they find safe investments that offer very little in the way of returns. It's either, "Hey, if I want to make money, I've got to put my money at risk," or "If I want to keep my money safe, I'm stuck with the bank CDs at 1 or 2 percent."

HYBRID PLANS: THE "BEST OF BOTH WORLDS" SOLUTION

What people need is a middle ground and that's where the hybrid world comes in play. With a hybrid investment plan, we use investments that give you the best of both worlds. The hybrid will give you the guaranteed protection of your principal that the banks are going to offer you, but they're also going to give you the opportunity to make money when the stock market goes up.

First, you need to understand that these investments cap the gains on the upside. A lot of these investments have a hard cap—which means you can't make more than 5 or 6 percent in a certain year—or they have a percentage or participation cap, which means you're only going to make 70 percent of the gain in the market. If the stock market's up 20 percent, you're not going to make 20 percent. It's not reasonable to think that you are going to get 100 percent of the stock market gains in good years, but none of the stock market losses in bad years. If someone tells you that they will give you all the gains and none of the losses, that's a Bernie Madoff thing. It's not possible.

Therefore, in good years, you're only going to make 5, 6 or 7 percent, or you're only going to make 70 percent of the market's gain. But when you give up some of the upside, what you get on the other side is that your principal is 100 percent guaranteed. You'll never lose money when the stock market goes down, and you still might be guaranteed, for example, to make 60 percent of the gains when the stock market goes up. In this case, if the stock market is up 10 percent, you'll make 6 percent, but when the stock market is down 10 percent, you're not going to lose anything. This type of investment is a way that you can have your cake and eat it too. You'll make some money when the stock market goes up, but you'll never lose a penny when the stock market goes down.

Basically, a hybrid plan will keep your principal safe; it has no downside (and has upside potential), and it has tax benefits. So what are these products and where do you get them? These products are annuities and they are sold by insurance companies.

A FIXED ANNUITY=SAFE MONEY

The first type of annuity is a fixed annuity that works in a similar fashion to a bank CD, although it is not FDIC-insured like a bank CD, but rather guaranteed by the insurance carrier. The fixed annuity will pay you a fixed amount of interest for a fixed number of years. It might be 3 percent guaranteed for five years, or 4 percent guaranteed for seven years, something with a fixed amount of interest for a fixed number of years.

A VARIABLE ANNUITY=OPPORTUNITY MONEY

On the other end of the spectrum is a variable annuity. In a variable annuity, you are basically putting your money in the stock market. When you give your money to the variable annuity company, you don't know what you're going to get back at the end of the day. If you put $100,000 in today and you cash it out five years from now, it might be worth $150,000 or it might be worth $50,000. You just don't know. When I talk to retirees, a lot of times people ask, "Well, why would I put my money in a variable annuity when I could have just put it into mutual funds?"

The reason is that a variable annuity has two advantages over a regular mutual fund. The first advantage is that the money will grow tax deferred while it's in there. If you put your money in a collection of mutual funds, you're going to pay taxes on that money every year whether you use it or not. But if you put it in the variable annuity, you're not going to pay tax on it until you actually take the money out. The tax deferral is one advantage of the variable annuity over just having money straight in the stock market.

The second advantage is that all variable annuities come with a death benefit. That death benefit guarantees that if you die while you're in the investment, your beneficiary will get at least what you put into it. If you put $100,000 in a variable annuity and five years later it's worth $50,000 and you want to cash out, you're only going to get the $50,000. But if you pass away, your beneficiary is going to get the original amount, $100,000. There is a guarantee on the death-benefit side with a variable annuity, but this guarantee confuses a lot of people. A lot of times when I talk to people about variable annuities, they say, "Well my advisor told me my principal is 100 percent guaranteed no matter what happens to the stock market." I have to point out to them that the guarantee only applies if you die.

If you try to cash it out while you're living, you're only going to get what it's worth.

The other downside of the variable annuity is that there are high internal expenses. Depending on the annuity company, those fees could be anywhere from 3 to 5 percent. That's how they guarantee the death benefit—the fees that they collect help offset the death benefit.

("BEST OF BOTH WORLDS" INVESTMENT)

We have the variable annuity on one side, and on the other side, the fixed annuity is plain vanilla, like a CD. Then we have the hybrid or the fixed index annuity, where your principal is going to be 100 percent guaranteed by the insurance carrier no matter what, and they usually guarantee a minimum interest as well. They say that no matter what happens to your account, you can never grow less than 1 percent. So there's a guaranteed minimum return that you'll get, even if the stock market's negative. It's never going to be just zero. You're always guaranteed to make something. Even if the stock market is down for 10 straight years, you'll get 1 percent a year for those 10 years, so it's better than just having it sit under your mattress. In the good years, you could make a percent of the market, perhaps between 5 and 8 percent. Fixed index annuities have historically averaged somewhere between 5 and 8 percent since their inception; these types investments were created around 1995. So they've been around for about 16 years, and looking back over these years they've averaged about 5 to 8 percent per year through good markets, bad markets, and flat markets.

Yes, there are fees on index annuities because, again, they have to have a cushion to guarantee your principal when the stock market is going down, but the average fees are generally less than 1 percent. The fee is going to be about nine-tenths of 1 percent—that's the average fee on the index annuity. By contrast, the average fee on a variable annuity is about 3.5 percent.

Since their creation in 1995, fixed index annuities have grown in popularity. This is something that didn't even exist in 1994, and last year $20 billion went into fixed index annuities. It's a huge industry now, as it should be, because there is a lot of value in these types of guaranteed investment products.

For many retirees, these products fall into that 75 percent of knowledge that we don't know we don't know. When I talk about fixed index annuities, one of the first responses I get it is, "How come I've never heard of this?"

In my opinion, one of the reasons you don't know about fixed index annuities is that the financial media and advertising are controlled by the big Wall Street firms—the major wire house firms. These are the 800-pound gorillas of the industry, and they are the ones that put a lot of advertising out there and have stories in the Wall Street Journal. These companies make their money by selling stocks, bonds, and mutual funds. All you hear about in the mainstream media are the products that these companies are putting out there.

I want retirees to look at fixed index annuities because it removes the risk of taking a fixed amount from a fluctuating portfolio. These annuities all have what's called an income rider, which lets you take a guaranteed amount of income no matter how long you live. Whether you live for 10 years or 40 years once the investment starts, the income is guaranteed for as long as you live. As we talked about at the beginning of this book, having your necessary income guaranteed for life is the goal of all retirement planning, and that is why you need to take a serious look at fixed index annuities.

How To Maximize Your Social Security Benefits

Chapter Eight

President Franklin Delano Roosevelt started Social Security in 1935 during the height of the Great Depression. At that time, so many people were out of work and incomes were so low, the government wanted to start some kind of system for people to have guaranteed income when they were retired.

Before Social Security, you were on your own. There was no benefit program for retirees. The point of Social Security was to start paying guaranteed lifetime retirement benefits to people once they turned age 65. One of the funny things about Social Security is that in 1935, life expectancy was 63. That's kind of typical of the government. They said you couldn't start collecting Social Security until you're 65, when they figured most people weren't going to be alive at that time to collect it. So the government said, "You pay into Social Security, you'll pay tax into it, but your benefits will be paid out to you tax-free for the rest of your life."

That's the reason you hear all these stories about the insolvency of Social Security. When it was set up, the average life expectancy was pretty close to the age when you started collecting the benefit. Now, with people living longer and longer, Social Security has to pay someone for much longer. Say someone retires at 62 and then lives till age 92, well, that's 30 years of payments that are coming out, and that's never what the government expected when this was put in place 75 years ago.

THE "62" DECISION

Social Security has changed over the years. Now you can apply as early as age 62 if you want, but if you do that, your benefit is going to be reduced by about 25 percent. Whatever your benefit is at your full retirement age (which is now age 66), if you start at age 62 that benefit is reduced by 25 percent. The reduction goes down by about 7.5 percent or about 7 percent a year until you reach age 66. About 70 percent of people who apply for Social Security do apply right at age 62. However, most people don't take the time to do any planning to see what the benefit of waiting is going to be. Every month after age 66 that you delay collecting, your benefit will go up a little bit and that higher benefit is going to be guaranteed to be paid out the rest of your life.

THE BREAK-EVEN POINT

The reason you get less if you start taking Social Security earlier than age 66 and more if you take it out later than age 66, is because actuarially it's supposed to come out to be the same. If you take it at 66, and you get the higher benefit, based on your life expectancy you should receive the same amount in benefits if you took it at age 62 with the lesser benefit. The break-even point right now is about age 78. Statistically, if you think you're going to live past age 78, if you have longevity in your family, then it's in your best interest to wait longer to receive benefits. Once you go past that break-even age, every month afterwards is just more money in your pocket. It's more favorable for you to collect benefits later rather than earlier. But most people don't take the time to do the calculation and determine if they should delay taking income or not. They just automatically start collecting benefits at age 62, which is not necessarily the right thing to do. With planning, if you delay it, you could end up ahead in the long run.

For example, let's take someone who would have retired at age 66, at their full retirement age. For an average person, that benefit is $2,230 per month. If they took that amount at age 62 instead, it would be $1,672 per month. Think about it. Age 66 is $2,230 per month. Age 62 is $1,672 per month. And age 70 is $2,787. That's an example of what the difference in income can be. It's a $1,100-a-month difference taking it at age 62 instead of waiting till age 70.

HOW TO CHOOSE THE RIGHT AGE TO START YOUR BENEFITS

So the next question is, "How do you know the right age to apply?" First, you have to take a look at what all your sources of income are, and then what your assets are. If you're going to delay taking Social Security—instead of taking it at age 62, you're going to take it at 66 (and not have that $1,600 a month coming in)—then you're going to have to get that money from somewhere else for the next four years. You have to do an analysis of your assets to see if you have any available to generate that money. There are a lot of different software programs, where you can sit down and plug in all the numbers, plug in your pension amount and your asset size, and the software program will create a nice analysis to tell you if it is worth waiting to collect Social Security. The AARP offers a helpful Social Security benefits calculator on its website (www.aarp.org) to help you make this decision.

HOW SOCIAL SECURITY'S COST OF LIVING ADJUSTMENT WORKS

Whether you apply at 62, 66, 67, or 70, the amount of your benefit when you apply will never change. The only thing that will change is the cost of living adjustment, or COLA, that the Social Security Administration applies to it. The cost of living adjustment is based on inflation rates and it changes every year. Back in 1980, for example, the Cost of Living Adjustment was 14.3 percent. In 1981 it was 11.2 percent. When you look at 2009, 2010 and 2011, you find that there wasn't a cost of living adjustment. The administration determined that based on the consumer price index, there was no inflation during the year. Your Social Security benefits will go up, but the amount of the increase is very unpredictable. That makes it difficult to plan for COLA. I usually use 2 or 3 percent a year as the COLA increase, just to have it built into the plan.

The key thing to understand is that once you start receiving Social Security benefits you will have the opportunity for those benefits to go up a little bit every year based on inflation. That's basically it, when it comes to COLA. There will be an increase in your benefits, as opposed to a pension from your employer. When that pension starts, in general, it never increases. If your pension starts at $1,500 a month, it's going to be $1,500 a month for life. With Social Security benefits, you expect some increases from year to year.

SOCIAL SECURITY AND YOUR SPOUSE

Let's talk about the traditional family, where the husband typically makes more than the wife. I don't mean to be sexist, but that's the reality for most of the retirees I talk to. In this traditional example, the husband is going to receive his Social Security benefit. Social Security benefits are based on earnings throughout the course of a lifetime, so if the wife has a work history in place, this couple is looking at two numbers. They look at what the wife's benefit would be based on her actual earnings, and then they look at what her husband is making. The wife is entitled to the greater of her own earnings or 50 percent of what her husband's benefit is.

To give you an example, let's say the husband is going to make $1,600 a month from Social Security based on his earnings. Based on the wife's earnings, she is going to make $500 a month. In this case, she would actually then be able to collect $800 a month because 50 percent of her husband's earnings is greater than what she would have earned on her own. Don't worry, this choice is made automatically by the Social Security Administration, so you can't really make a mistake on this one.

HOW DEATH AND DIVORCE AFFECTS YOUR SOCIAL SECURITY BENEFITS

As I mentioned earlier, if someone is widowed before the age of 62, they could apply for Social Security benefits at age 60. If a female is a widow at age 55, she still can't receive Social Security benefits until she turns 60, but she will not have to wait until age 62. She'll be able to take her benefits two years earlier, but she will have to apply for them. The government is not going to automatically start making those payments to her at age 60 because she is a widow. She would have to apply early for that.

More and more, I hear questions about the effect of divorce on benefits because divorce is becoming more prevalent in our society. Here's how it works. If a marriage lasts at least 10 years and a person has not remarried, then they're going to be entitled to spousal benefits based on their spouse's earnings, if those earnings are higher than their own earnings. As I mentioned before, you're entitled to earnings either based on your own work record or your spouse's, whichever is higher. The same would happen if you're divorced. You have the same option if your ex-husband is a high earner—your benefit could be half of his total.

CAN YOU WORK AND STILL COLLECT SOCIAL SECURITY BENEFITS?

Let's talk about how working affects benefits. If you apply at age 62, which is considered early retirement, there are restrictions on how much income you can earn before your Social Security income is affected. In 2012, the earnings test is $14,160. That means if you're collecting early Social Security before age 66, you can earn up to $14,160 a year before your Social Security is affected. Any income you make beyond $14,160 affects your Social Security benefits. How? It's a pretty simple formula. For every two dollars you earn above $14,160, a dollar of benefits is going to be withheld from your Social Security payment. That $14,160 earnings ceiling can help you make the decision whether you should apply for Social Security at age 62. If you're still working and making $20,000 or $30,000 a year, then it's a no brainer that you're not going to apply for Social Security at age 62. You're going to lose a lot of those benefits anyway because of the earnings test. But if you're not working, or you're working part time and you're only making $5,000 or $10,000 per year, then it's not a cut-and-dried decision. You can make up to $14,160 without having to pay back Social Security benefits.

Keep in mind that the $14,160 doesn't include pension income or IRA income—it's solely based on W2 wages.

When you're 66, you don't have the income ceiling because you've reached full retirement age. You can continue to earn income without it affecting your benefits. I keep talking about age 66, because that's the full retirement age for most of my clients. If you're younger, that's not the case. I'm 45 years old, and my full retirement age is 67 and 3 months, and for younger people, it's even older than that. For most people who are retired or are considering retirement now, 66 is still the age. If you're one of those people, once you reach the full retirement age of 66, you can make as much W2 income as you want and not have it affect your Social Security benefits.

Your pension income does not affect your Social Security benefits regarding how much you can collect. However, that income does affect you in how much you are taxed. Again, going back to 1935, when Social Security was first created, the government said you'll get your Social Security benefits tax-free for life. Like everything else in the government, things change. In 1983, Congress passed a law that said, depending on how much you earn, as much as 50 percent of your Social Security benefits are subject to taxation. At that time, the threshold was that if you were a single filer and you were making above $25,000 of provisional income, then 50 percent of your benefits would be taxed. If you were a married couple making above $32,000 in provisional income, 50 percent of your Social Security benefits would be taxed.

In 1993, Congress passed another law regarding taxation of Social Security benefits. This time, they added a second layer, saying that if you're a single filer making above $34,000 of provisional income, then 85 percent of your Social Security benefits will be taxed. If you were a married couple making above $44,000, then 85 percent of your Social Security benefits would be taxed.

WHAT IS "PROVISIONAL INCOME"?

The next question you are probably asking is, "What's provisional income?" Provisional income is basically everything you make. Provisional income includes your W2 wages, your interest income, your dividend income, your pension income, your IRA distributions, and it even includes your tax-free dividends and interest. If you have municipal bonds, those are tax-free on the federal level, but those dividends are still counted into provisional income. They even count 50 percent of your Social Security income as part of your provisional income. Again, you can see the strange way government thinks; they count 50 percent of your Social Security income into the formula that determines if Social Security is taxable.

HOW TAX PLANNING CAN HELP YOU KEEP MORE OF YOUR MONEY

With all these sources contributing to provisional income, you can see that getting to $25,000 as a single filer or $32,000 as a married couple is not that hard, especially when so much goes into the formula to determine if Social Security is taxable. Being aware of this formula is also an opportunity for tax planning, where you can possibly control some of the taxable interest, and some of the dividends. If you can control those sources, that makes tax planning easier. The goal is to see if you can possibly keep your Social Security from being taxed with proper planning.

Let's go back to George and Shirley, the couple who were receiving about $40,000 of interest from their CDs and dividends from their stocks, and how that entire $40,000 was showing up on their tax return. However, if we use some tax-efficient investments, George and Shirley are still getting $40,000 of income in their pocket. Because of the exclusion ratio of some investments, all of that $40,000 isn't showing up on their tax return—only about $8,000 is showing up on their tax return. So George and Shirley are still getting the same $40,000 in their pocket, but they don't have to pay tax on that whole amount, which caused a substantial decrease in their provisional income. Before we employed those tax-planning strategies, George and Shirley were in a situation where they were taxed on some of their Social Security benefits. We were able to change that, so that none of their Social Security benefits was taxed.

TWO IMPORTANT LINES TO LOOK AT ON YOUR TAX RETURN.

When you look at your tax return, you want to look at the items that you can control. Obviously the money that you're getting from Social Security income is something you can't control, because you're not going to tell the government to send you less in your Social Security check each month. The money that you're getting from your pension is something you can't control, because again, you're not going to tell your former employer to send you less money. They would love to hear that, of course, but you won't be making that call. So those are the numbers you cannot control. But when you look at interest income, which is Line 8, or if you look at dividend income, which is Line 9, those are numbers you can control. And if they're very high, you can look at strategies to have those numbers either reduced or eliminated.

That's really the simple lesson of tax planning. Look at Line 8 and 9 of your tax return. If there are large numbers on those lines, then that is usually a pretty good indication that there is an opportunity to explore tax-reduction strategies.

I can't stress enough how important it is to know about Social Security income: How it works, how it's distributed, and how it's taxed because this is something that's going to affect the amount of income you have for the rest of your life. With people living longer and longer, you have to think about maximizing that benefit. If you're going to live until your mid- to late 80s or even early 90s, you want to make the most out of that Social Security benefit. Automatically taking it at age 62 is not the way to maximize your benefit. You want to sit down with a retirement planner who understands all the ins and outs of Social Security benefits to determine the optimal time to take those benefits.

The biggest mistake I see when it comes to Social Security benefits is when someone just automatically takes the benefit at age 62, without an analysis of his or her whole situation. That person could optimize benefits by taking them at a different time. The mistake is assuming that age 62 is the right time, no matter what.

If you would like to learn more about Social Security benefits, please visit www.ssa.gov.

Long Term Care Insurance That Makes Sense

Chapter Nine

Are you worried about losing your assets if you have to go into a nursing home? Do you have long-term-care insurance? If you don't, what's the biggest reason you didn't buy long-term-care insurance? It's probably the "use it or lose it" risk. Most people don't want to pay a significant amount of money for something they might never use.

There are some long-term-care programs available where if you don't use them, you can either get all of your money back, or your beneficiaries get the money in the form of a tax-free death benefit. In this chapter, I will show you how they work and how to tell which plan is the right match for you.

I've been working with retirees for 20 years, and one of the biggest concerns that they have—the one thing that comes up almost all the time—is the fear of what's going to happen to their money if they need to go into a nursing home. People tell me, "I don't want to lose my house if I go into a nursing home, and I don't want to have to spend all my assets if I go into a nursing home." Everybody has heard horror stories of people who go to a nursing home and spend two, three, four, or even five hundred thousand dollars of their assets and basically go broke. Nobody wants to do that. People would rather give that money to the kids. In truth, they'd rather it go anywhere than to the nursing home. Most people know that the way to beat that fear is to have long-term-care insurance. The irony is that very few people have it, even though so many people are concerned about the risk of long-term care.

The big problem with traditional long-term-care insurance is that it's "use it or lose it." If you never require long-term care at a nursing home, then all those premiums you have paid over the years were wasted. That's a valid concern. For example, if you pay $5,000 per year for 20 years of long-term-care insurance and you never use that insurance, you've basically wasted that $100,000. This "use it or lose it" risk keeps people from thinking seriously about long-term-care insurance. I want to show you that you have insurance options that will offer you a benefit even if you never need long-term care.

ALTERNATIVES TO "USE IT OR LOSE IT" INSURANCE

Until eight or 10 years ago, the traditional, "use it or lose it" insurance was the only option for long-term-care insurance. Insurance companies have gotten innovative and they have come up with ways to overcome this "use it or lose it" risk, but most people are still not aware of these alternatives. Today, you have more sensible options for long-term-care insurance which deserve a long, hard look.

THE "RETURN OF PREMIUM" SOLUTION

There are two ways to ensure or protect your assets from long-term-care expenses. The first way is the return-of-premium solution and the second way is the 1 percent solution. The return-of-premium solution makes sense for certain individuals who already have a lot of money set aside for potential long-term-care expenses. Very often, when I go through a retiree's financial situation and see where their money is and where their income comes from, I'll come across someone who may have $50,000 or $100,000 that's set off on the side in a separate bank account. They aren't saying it's their rainy day fund or their grandchildren's college fund. They haven't defined it. I'll ask, "What is this money for?" They say, "Well, that's the money I'm going to use if I ever need to go into a nursing home. That's how I'm going to pay for it."

I understand their thinking, but then I'll ask, "Okay, so how long is this $50,000 going to last if you require nursing-home care?" They think it might only last a year or two, based on what prices may be. This is when I say, "Let me show you a way to leverage this amount of money you have already set aside, to get you more than one or two years' worth of coverage."

THE THREE BUCKETS OF MONEY

Just setting aside $50,000 is not a valid plan for long-term-care insurance. First, that $50,000 is probably not going to come close to covering your care if you really do need nursing-home care. Second, that money could do a lot more for you if you invested it with an insurance company than it does sitting in a CD. Instead, think about taking that $50,000 and giving it to an insurance company in a lump sum. When you give this money to the insurance company, you create three buckets of money. Let me explain.

The first bucket is your liquidity bucket. The $50,000 that you give to the insurance company is always liquid to you if you ever change your mind about your coverage. Whether it's six months or six years from now, if you ever say to the insurance company, "You know what? I need that $50,000 back, I have to do something different with it," you're guaranteed 100 percent of your money back. You basically have the same liquidity that you have with a CD. Right now the CD is liquid; if you give it to the insurance company it's still liquid there. You have not given up any liquidity whatsoever.

The second bucket of money that you create is what's called your death benefit. Let's imagine this $50,000 investment is for a 65-year-old female. That second bucket, the death benefit, means that if she passes away and never needed any kind of long-term-care insurance, her beneficiaries are going to get $87,000, tax-free. Compare that to if she just had that money sitting in the CD. Maybe it grew a little bit over the years and it was worth $60,000 when she died. The $60,000 still goes to her beneficiaries, but they're going to be taxed on it.

The third bucket is called the long-term-care bucket. In this example, we're also looking at a 65-year-old woman who has invested $50,000. If she needed long-term care, her $50,000 would now give her $175,000 to spend on long-term care. If she was just spending for long-term care out of the CD, she'd only have $50,000. With the third bucket, she more than triples the amount of money she has available for long-term care. It goes from $50,000 to $175,000 to pay for it.

Let's go back to the example of the person who keeps the $50,000 in a CD,

as opposed to buying long-term-care insurance. He keeps the money in a CD and in the back of his mind it's for long-term-care insurance. Let's say he lives for 10 more years and then passes away; he never needed any coverage. Then let's look at the value of that CD. In 10 years, maybe it would grow to $55,000. In this case, the beneficiaries would get the $55,000 in the CD, but they'd have to pay tax on it. If he had chosen the return-of-premium solution, his beneficiaries would get $80,000, completely tax-free. That's assuming he died without needing coverage.

On the other side, if he does need long-term-care coverage and never chose the return-of-premium solution, he's just going to take money from the CD until it's gone. He is only going to get $50,000, $55,000 or $60,000 worth of coverage for however long the money lasts. If he took it from the long-term-care insurance, he would have $175,000 to spend on coverage, rather than just whatever the balance in that CD was.

The first thing I hear, when I tell people about this, is that it sounds too good to be true. Well, it is true. The only catch is that you have to qualify. Like most life insurance, not everybody can get it. The insurance company will do a phone interview and ask you a lot of medical questions to make sure you're in good shape. They don't want to insure you, in this example, for $87,000 if you have a pre-existing condition that may kill you in a couple years. The catch is that you have to qualify medically for it, but if you qualify, this insurance is a no-brainer because the benefits far outweigh any costs and risks associated with the coverage. If you ever want to change your mind, it has the 100 percent money-back guarantee.

Different companies have different terms for their specific products, but in general, I refer to them as return-of-premium solutions so it doesn't sound like a specific product push. What I'm talking about is more of a concept or a strategy, not any one specific product.

Needless to say, these return-of-premium solution products are incredibly popular with retirees. The only problem is that only about 50 percent of the people who apply are approved because of the health criteria. Ask your retirement-planning advisor about these plans and find out if you qualify as soon as you can.

RETURN OF PREMIUM SOLUTION: THREE BUCKETS OF MONEY

For a $50,000 Policy...

Bucket 1: $50,000, always liquid

Bucket 2: $87,000, death benefit

Bucket 3: $175,000, long-term-care protection

THE 1 PERCENT SOLUTION

The 1 percent solution is for the situations where someone would say either, "I don't have a big lump sum of money that I can give to the insurance company right now," or "I don't want to give a lump sum to the insurance company. I'd rather go the more traditional route of pay as you go and pay the monthly or yearly premium. However, I want to avoid the use-it-or-lose-it problem."

For the 1 percent solution, I look at someone's situation and examine the entire nest egg. For example, let's say a couple have $350,000 in their nest egg. I'll say to them, "Let's take 1 percent of that nest egg." That's an easy number for people to get their minds around. They think, "It's only 1 percent, that's nothing." We take the 1 percent of that $350,000 ($3,500) and give it to the insurance company. It's very similar to the traditional long-term-care insurance where you're paying the insurance company an annual premium and you have to pay that annual premium for the rest of your life.

The benefit that you get from that annual premium may be very similar to traditional long-term-care insurance. For the traditional insurance, the company says, "You give us X amount of dollars and we'll guarantee you $200,000 of benefits that you can have available to you over your lifetime." The same thing happens with the 1 percent solution. The insurance companies say, for example, "You give us X amount of dollars and we'll give you $150,000 of long-term-care benefits." The difference with the 1 percent solution is that in the old scenario or the traditional scenario, if you die without ever needing coverage you get nothing for all those premiums that you put in. With the 1 percent solution, if you die and you never needed coverage, then your beneficiary is going to get a tax-free death benefit.

If you have $150,000 available for long-term care and you never need it, then that $150,000 is going to go to your beneficiaries in the form of a tax-free life-insurance death benefit. The "use it or lose it" problem is eliminated because somebody's going to get this money back. Somehow, some way, somebody is getting that money back. Either you're getting it back in the form of long-term-care payments, or your beneficiary is getting it back in the form of a tax-free death benefit, which also then helps lower the taxable estate inherited from you. It's a win-win situation for everybody involved.

To better understand how the 1 percent solution compares to traditional long-term-care insurance, let's say a woman pays $5,000 a year for the traditional policy. The insurance company tells her, "We'll give you $352,000 for long-term care, should you need it." She's 61 years old, so if she has a 25-year life expectancy, she could be paying $5,000 a year for 25 years. That means she will have paid $125,000 in out-of-pocket money into this policy. With the traditional policy, if she passes away and she never needed that coverage, that $125,000 is basically gone. She never used the coverage, so it was wasted. With the 1 percent solution, the scenario plays out differently. Again, she lives 25 years, pays out $125,000, but never needs the coverage. Instead of being wasted, that money turns into a tax-free $352,000 paid out to her beneficiary. She never has to feel as if she's paid all that money all those years and received no benefit. Her beneficiary gets a boatload of tax-free money. On the other hand, if she had needed long-term care, she would have had $352,000 to spend for it.

Again, when I explain the 1 percent solution to retirees they say the same thing, "It's too good to be true." But it absolutely is true, with two caveats. First, you have to be able to afford whatever that premium is every year, whether it's $3,000, $5,000 or $10,000 per year. Whatever you commit to, you have to be able to pay that year in and year out. If you aren't able to pay one year, the policy lapses and then all your money is wasted. You have to be able to afford the payment. That is paramount. The second caveat, again, is the health issue. You have to qualify for this insurance because the insurance company is not going to insure just anybody. It wants to make sure you're healthy enough for the coverage.

THE 1 PERCENT SOLUTION: TWO BUCKETS OF MONEY

For annual $3,500* premium to life insurance company

Bucket 1: $50,000, always liquid

Bucket 2: $87,000, death benefit

*premium amount will vary

If you can afford it, I definitely advise you to hold some type of insurance for long-term-care, because those costs can eat away your assets if you're not protected.

CHAPTER 10

How To Get The Most From Your Life Insurance

Chapter Ten

D
o you have a life insurance policy that is at least five years old? If so, what is the cash value? How would you like to be able to take the cash value of that existing policy and possibly double, triple, or even quadruple the coverage with no out-of-pocket costs to you? Let me show you how.

If you have life-insurance policies that are at least five years old, you should take a look at them to see if there are ways to improve on them. Insurance companies are always coming up with innovations and new ways to lower the cost of insurance, and they are always competing with other companies. Like a lot of commodities out there, life insurance is getting cheaper and cheaper these days. You can compare it to stock commissions 20 or 30 years ago. The only way to buy a stock was to go through a stockbroker, and you had to pay on average $200, $300 or even $400 per trade. Now you buy stocks online for $6 a trade because it's considered a commodity. Life insurance is considered a commodity too. You can get it anywhere.

Always take a look at your existing coverage and see if there's a way to improve it. Keep in mind that we're only talking about cash-value life insurance; in other words, life insurance with a savings component. If you have term insurance—typically, less expensive coverage that offers a death benefit over a specified term with no saving component—then there's really no way to improve upon it. But if you have cash-value insurance, you might have options to save. First, find out the cash value and the death benefit of your current policy, and then see if you can get more coverage by using the cash value of your existing coverage and transferring to a new company.

For example, I had a client who came to me a couple years ago, and he had a $100,000 cash-value policy with a $125,000 death benefit, and he was paying $1,000 per year of premium. His question was should he just cancel the policy, he was sick of paying the $1,000, and take the cash value out. I was able to show him that by taking that existing cash value and transferring it to a new company, he was able to increase his death benefit from $125,000 to $278,000. He was also able to eliminate the annual premium. He wouldn't have to pay any more money out of pocket, and his death benefit more than doubled.

Most people don't realize there are options to reprice their old insurance. If you don't search out these options, you could be leaving money on the table.

APPLY FOR THE INSURANCE FIRST, THEN MAKE YOUR DECISION

If you're not sure if you should apply for the long-term-care insurance, or should switch out the coverage, the first thing you should do is apply. Find out if the insurance company will even insure you or make you an offer. Most people get caught up in what I call "analysis paralysis," where they think about it too long. "Should I do it, should I not?" I say, "You may not even get approved for the coverage." When I sit down with individuals, I give them my best guess, based on their age and their gender, of what they would qualify for. These examples that I'm giving are based on general guidelines. The insurance company itself is going to make a specific offer to you based on your specific health history.

Let's look again at that example of my client who turned his $125,000 death benefit into a $278,000 death benefit and eliminated his premium. My client was a 60-year-old male, and he was in good health. If he was in poor health, the insurance company may have declined him or may have offered a lot less than the $278,000. On the flip side, if he was in exceptional health, the insurance company might have offered more than the $278,000.

I always tell retirees, "Let's just put the application in." The application is not going to cost you anything, and it's not going to obligate you to do anything. It's just going to give you a solid offer or no offer from the insurance company. Once you get that actual offer in place from the insurance company, then we can sit down and analyze it to say, "Hey, this is something we absolutely should do because it's worth it," or "It's not worth it." You shouldn't agonize over a decision based on a general illustration; you should get a hard offer from the insurance company first and then make your decision.

LIFE INSURANCE REVIEW

	Old Policy	New Policy
Cash Value	$100,000*	$100,000
Death Benefit	$125,000	$278,186
Annual Premium	$1,000	$0

*actual amount will vary

Final Thoughts

People talk to me about their retirement for many reasons, but everybody is concerned about something. Some are concerned about what happens if they go into a nursing home and how they could lose all their money. Others are concerned about the amount of taxes that they're paying every year. Some people worry that their portfolio is going down in value every year and they will run out of money. They all have a specific concern that keeps them up at night and has them breaking into a cold sweat. If that's you, then you need to address your concerns. If you do nothing, whatever your particular concern is, it's not going to go away on its own. You have to do something to make that concern go away. You have to take action so you can start sleeping through the night without worrying.

THE DEFINITION OF FINANCIAL INSANITY

I always say, "The definition of financial insanity is doing the same thing, and expecting your situation to change." If nothing else, I hope this book has convinced you that it's time to act and talk to a retirement-planning specialist to take care of your concerns.

The key concepts I want you to take away from this book are that you need a retirement plan that focuses on lowering your risk, increasing your income, and reducing your taxes and fees. There are many options out there to improve your situation. Like many retirees, you may feel scared, but you need not think the stock market is your only alternative to the banks with their low CD rates.

As this book has shown, you have to be aware that there are many options available to increase your income, just like there are a lot of options out there to reduce your taxes and to limit your risk. You just have to know where to look. The problem is that the traditional places where people are looking—the brokerage houses, and the banks—don't have the answers they want. That doesn't mean the answers aren't out there somewhere. Use this book as a road map to find them.

Knowledge really is power, and most of it—75 percent, remember?—is knowledge we don't even know we don't know. Most people just don't know that they have alternatives to get long-term-care insurance without having to buy the traditional "use it or lose it" policies. Most don't know that you can make money in the stock market without putting yourself at risk. I often remind people that just because they haven't found the answer in one place doesn't mean the solution isn't out there somewhere.

What road are you on? If it isn't taking you in the right direction, then you need to take another road. In other words, if you're not comfortable with your current retirement plan, look at doing something different to get you to your destination, which in retirement is the same for everyone: peace of mind.

How do you know if you're on the right road? Talk to a competent retirement specialist. Don't just count on one of the many financial generalists out there. You need to talk to someone who specializes in retirement planning and that's all they do. If you were diagnosed with cancer, you'd go to a specialist, not your family doctor. Likewise, if you have retirement concerns, don't keep going to the person at the bank or the traditional stockbroker; you want to go to a retirement specialist who is uniquely qualified in those areas. Retirement has become extremely complicated, and your accountant and your broker don't have the expertise you need.

At the beginning of this book, I pointed out that when you're working, you're not concerned about the stock market's fluctuations because your paycheck is what defines your lifestyle. Your paycheck puts food on the table and pays the mortgage and the cable bill and all those other expenses. Your paycheck dictates your lifestyle while you're working. Once you're retired, your retirement income will dictate your lifestyle. It's not the amount of assets that you have, per se, but it's the amount of income that you can derive from your assets that is going to determine your lifestyle.

YOU MUST REMEMBER THIS

If you take one thing away from this book, please remember that when you approach and eventually enter your retirement, you are moving from the accumulation phase of your financial life to the preservation and distribution phase of your life. That requires a serious change of mind-set. That's the marathoner's mind-set. Months before race day, smart marathon runners will train hard to make sure they are prepared for anything that can come up that day. That is how you minimize risk in a race. You should have that same mind set and strategy as you prepare for your retirement. You need to avoid all risks now because the money you've saved is going to fund your retirement. It can be done by employing tax-reduction strategies, avoiding fees, and finding safe investment vehicles like fixed index annuities.

Is this the most exciting plan? Of course not. But it is a plan that provides safety and the highest income stream that you and your spouse cannot outlive. When it comes to your retirement, at the end of the race, boring wins every time.

How can you use this book?

MOTIVATE

EDUCATE

THANK

INSPIRE

PROMOTE

CONNECT

Why have a custom version of *Retirement Is A Marathon, Not A Sprint?*

- Build personal bonds with customers, prospects, employees, donors, and key constituencies
- Develop a long-lasting reminder of your event, milestone, or celebration
- Provide a keepsake that inspires change in behavior and change in lives
- Deliver the ultimate "thank you" gift that remains on coffee tables and bookshelves
- Generate the "wow" factor

Books are thoughtful gifts that provide a genuine sentiment that other promotional items cannot express. They promote employee discussions and interaction, reinforce an event's meaning or location, and they make a lasting impression. Use your book to say "Thank You" and show people that you care.

Retirement Is A Marathon, Not A Sprint is available in bulk quantities and in customized versions at special discounts for corporate, institutional, and educational purposes. To learn more please contact our Special Sales team at:

1.866.775.1696 • sales@advantageww.com • www.AdvantageSpecialSales.com